<18>

Faith for the Next Generation

By Bob Lenz and Rich Melheim

with Jenica Halula

"Then you can tell the Next Generation detail by detail the story of God…"

Psalm 48:13b-14 MSG

The symbol of "<18>" signifies our mission to transform the lives of youth with the hope of Jesus while they are under (<) 18 years of age to set a spiritual path for their lives over (>) 18.

<18> FAITH FOR THE NEW GENERATION

First edition. Published by Life Promotions, Inc.,
Neenah, Wisconsin, 2017

All emphasis within Scripture is the authors' own.

ISBN: 978-0-9856716-9-3 Paperback
ISBN: 978-0-9975440-0-8 e-book

Library of Congress Control Number: 2017940691

Printed in the United States of America

Life Promotions, Inc.

2030 American Drive
Neenah, Wisconsin 54956
info@lifepromotions.com

<18> FAITH FOR THE NEXT GENERATION

Table of Contents

ACKNOWLEDGEMENTS

To Mom and Dad,

who taught me how to live and die

and live.

Rich Melheim

Dedicated to my 5 kids and 10 grandchildren.

May you find faith in your generation and pass it on to your children

and your children's children.

Dedicated to every parent and grandparent

whose heart aches to see their kids and grandkids come to faith.

Bob Lenz

BEFORE WE BEGIN

#BobLenz #RichMelheim

During the writing of this book Rich would lead us in prayer, firmly grasping the hands of those next to him, until we were all gathered in a beautiful circle. This way of prayer reflected care, order, and the value of each member. Later, Bob — without warning while driving the car or writing on a white board — would begin praying. He would begin speaking to God, reflecting the nearness of God in each moment, and the intimacy of God's friendship with us.

While driving through Aspen one morning on our writing retreat, Bob was so deep in verbal prayer that he didn't notice he was speeding. We got pulled over. Laughing and joking with the police officer while trying to explain, Bob struck up a faith conversation. We ended up praying with the officer before driving on. (And yes, he still got the ticket!)

We express our faith in both structure and spontaneity. This book is written in the voice of a conversation, rather than a formal piece of literature. We are breaking with conventional writing norms to engage you with us, and with the thoughts in your own head, in a way that will start other conversations with people you know and value. We are writing this in a way that we hope will make you feel like you are sitting at a dining room table or on a deck with us in the cool night breeze talking with friends. Laughing. Maybe tearing up a little. Listening to one another. Listening to the voice of God speaking to and through each other.

WE WANT TO ENCOURAGE SIMPLE, HELPFUL STRUCTURE IN THIS BOOK. HABITS THAT WILL HOLD US WHEN WE CANNOT HOLD OURSELVES.

We want to encourage simple, helpful structure in this book. **Habits that will hold us** when we cannot hold ourselves. And we want to encourage you to **stay engaged so you'll recognize these spontaneous moments** that seem to appear out of nowhere. These moments are ripe for life-changing action and conversation. Both structure and flexibility are important.

Both of these must be **rooted in love**. In these pages, we hope to rekindle that fire in all of our hearts. We believe we're made for love.

The authors of this book share a familiarity and deep affection for many different expressions of the Christian faith. We do not agree on everything, but we stand united and focus on what we passionately agree on: the importance of passing our faith on to the Next Generation.

We want to give you **hope**. We stand a few years farther down this journey, and we can call back to you some encouragement and advice about what we have learned.

Last, but not least, we want to set before you a **challenge**. All our children are now past the age of eighteen. They are still our "babies" even though they are adults. And we have buried every one of our parents. We will always be their children, even though they are physically absent. We stand here with a perspective that is hard to get in the middle of the sleepless nights and soccer practices. It is so easy to let the urgent needs outweigh the eternal. We let the best fall to the side while we're giving our children all the rest.

In this book we'll talk about ways you can pass on your faith during the normal days, the sad days, and the best days. Whether you are a parent, an aunt, a teacher, a mentor, a big brother, a surrogate grandpa or a coach, there is something here for you. The kids out there need you.

So welcome to the conversation. Welcome to our thoughts. Welcome to <18>. Welcome to our hearts and prayers and hopes for you in your faith journey. Take the advice or leave it. Learn from it or remove the slivers of gold you find in between the pages and melt them down into something beautiful you can fashion for your life. Our hope, our prayer, our joy, our dream is that this conversation between friends becomes the beginning of a world of beauty, depth, wonder and joy between you and the people you love the most.

The people who will walk from your grave one day will be better, stronger and more faithful just because you were there for them.

PART 1

Why should we share the Good News?

WHY <18>?

#BobLenz

When I speak at events all over the world, people will introduce me in various ways. Once the introduction went something like this, "Bob Lenz speaks to half a million students each year in all fifty states and twenty-five countries. He's authored four books, and he runs a music festival called Lifest. . . . I knew Bob when he was *still speaking to junior high kids.* Please welcome Bob Lenz."

I know he was trying to be nice. He was trying to say, "*Bob's gotten a little better. Now we can trust him with a real audience: Adults!*"

Don't get me wrong, I don't mind speaking to adults. They're not so bad once you get to know them! But I've started to get indignant when people ask me why I still speak to youth.

Two out of three people who come to Christ do so before the age of 18.[1] That's why I still speak to youth. Yet, as I travel across the country, I meet a lot of youth directors who see youth ministry as a stepping stone to "real ministry." Let me tell you, this is not a stepping stone. It is the foundation. It matters.

If you owned a company and two-thirds of your business came from one demographic or customer base would you ignore that group? Of course not. Would you just tolerate that area? Of course not. Wouldn't you focus on it? Invest in it? Wouldn't you give everything you could for that area?

How many of the adults that "real ministry" is aimed toward were the very same people marginalized by the church in their childhood or youth? I think we should pour our prime resources into preventing forest fires rather than only on putting them out.

I was at a church a few years ago, and they told me they had about two hundred people at the service. I said "Really? It looked like a lot more than that."

They replied, "Oh, yeah, but we don't count children."

I said, "You don't count children? Why not?"

Don't they know where adults come from? Maybe they think new adults simply appear fully formed.

We might be having discussions about when or how to teach our children where babies come from, but maybe we need to start explaining to adults where *they* come from: everyone was a child once, and that childhood isn't cut off from our adulthood; it's the foundation for it. Children are creating memories and habits and abilities that will last their entire lifetime. They feel hope, and joy, and pain, and those memories inform their life choices.

Children are forming their ideas about the existence of real forgiveness. Can love exist without strings attached? Through the experiences of these early years they will conclude whether they are worthy of love and whether there is anything meaningful and satisfying in this fast-paced, consuming world. Of course, we can change the ideas we form in our earliest years, but that typically requires years of intentional work and often therapy.

Our God counts children. In fact, God doesn't just count them by number. He calls them by name.

I was at another church, and I asked, "Why do you have kids' church? Why do you release the kids?"

"So that the adults can enjoy the service."

"So you release them because it's babysitting," I commented.

"No, no," they corrected me, "It's *free* babysitting."

Please hear me. I know not all churches view it this way. I know many churches release the children because they believe they are partnering with the parents whose number-one responsibility is to raise them in the faith. It's so encouraging to see that, but I know how easy it is in this world to go back to thinking that kids are just not as important as adults.

There is a really good musician who goes to my church, who plays at many community events. He came to me and said, "Bob, I really feel like God wants me to start sharing my gift for his kingdom. I want to start playing worship music at church."

I told him that was awesome!

He said, "That's what I thought! But when I talked to the elders, they wouldn't even let me play on a Sunday morning on the stage. They said I have to play for the children's church. What an insult."

He said that to the wrong guy!

I looked at him and said, "*An insult*? What a privilege. What an opportunity. What a responsibility."

If we want more than eulogies and marble headstones in our churches, then we must engage with the rough edges of youth and childhood. We must share Jesus with them today.

Let's look at another <18>. Luke **18**:16.

Jesus called the children to himself and said, "Let the children come to me, and do not hinder them, for the kingdom of God belongs to the ***Elders***."

Sorry, that's not right.

"The kingdom of God belongs to the ***ordained.***"

Whoops.

"The kingdom of God belongs to the ***paid staff.***"

Let me try one more time.

"The kingdom of God belongs to the ***biggest financial donor***."

No.

"The kingdom of God belongs to these, the ***children***."

That's the one! That is the backwards, mixed-up thing Jesus says!

> Luke 18:16:
>
> "But Jesus called the children to him and said,
> 'Let the little children come to me,
> and do not hinder them,
> for the kingdom of God belongs to such as these.'"

So here's the premise of this book: Kids and youth are ready to hear the good news right now. There is nothing more important than our youth coming to know God. Will we see the value of these people that God calls valuable? We don't want to gain the whole world and lose our families in the process. Will *we* share the Good News with them?

CEMENT

#RichMelheim

My very first job was resetting basement floors. We'd hack up the old cement floor with sledgehammers, shovel the pieces out of the basement windows, and then pour in the new floor.

"THE LONGER IT SETS, THE HARDER IT GETS"

My boss would tell me to work quickly.

"The longer it sets, the harder it gets," he'd always say.

Children's lives are like wet cement. This is the time in life when deep and lasting impressions are being made on their self-image, habits and abilities. Neurology tells us that the anchors that are set in place before puberty will stand the test of time. The things we learn and memorize before puberty get set in our brain in a way that is much more difficult after puberty.

This has been called the Kissinger Effect.[2]

Henry Kissinger and his younger brother moved to the United States from Germany when they were age twelve and ten. They both learned English upon moving to the U.S., but Henry could not shake his thick German accent, even as an adult. His younger brother, on the other hand, who was only *two years* younger than him, spoke English without an accent. His brother learned English while the cement was wet, and Henry learned it when the cement had already begun to set. The Kissinger Effect shows us how receptive the young brain is.

After we poured the new cement into the basement, we would smooth it out just right and then leave for the day. If I'd snuck back into the house that night with some friends, we could have easily damaged that cement with nothing but a toy sand shovel. Yet if I'd waited a year to return, I could have hacked at it for hours with a real shovel and done very little damage, except for bruising and blistering on my own hands.

Even strong-willed children and rebellious youth are having impressions pressed into them. They are getting an impression about if they are loved, if they matter to anyone, and if they have anything to offer this world.

In the teenage years, the cement is already setting, but this is not the time to abandon your children. Don't mirror them by throwing up your arms and storming away from a difficult situation. Their brains are rewiring during these years, and they need a secure foundation, even as they gain their independence. Which is, after all, what we want, right? We want them to become independent. The goal is to raise an adult; not to raise a child.

"What you believe by the time you are thirteen is what you will die believing," researcher George Barna has noted.[3]

A seven-year-old is not just learning how to spell 'right' and 'wrong,' but literally learning the deep meaning of what is good and what is bad. It is being cemented into their hearts in these years.

Bob and I believe that having a moral code (a set of rules which create a standard for your choices in life) is a good idea. This happens to be an intersection where science, social sciences, and religion all agree: structure and values make for healthier kids. I'm not saying we all agree on *which values* are important, but even the most public of public education wants to instill some values into kids:

Don't damage someone else's property. Be responsible for your own property. Don't hurt someone else with your words or your body.

That's all great stuff. Ultimately, having a structure that is a guide for our life decisions makes us happier than living on a whim and doing whatever we want to do in each moment. But I don't want my kids to *just* be happy. I want them to know joy.

This book isn't going to describe <18> experiences that will make our kids *happier.*

This book is about introducing God to our kids. And our kids to God.

Good morals aren't the most important thing they'll need. No matter how wonderful a person they become, the world is still going to knock them around. We all will be hurt, and no matter how hard we try not to, we will hurt others.

And whether we are young or old when we finally realize it: we have limited time on this planet. I want to give my kids the tools to face these complex and troubling issues as they grow up.

I want to give them something that will be useful when they've been crushed by external forces or are in despair over deep regrets. I want them to have something that won't crumble when they are, heaven forbid, sitting at the bedside of a friend who has cancer. I want them to have something that offers hope in both the highest joys they experience and the lowest sorrows.

A dream job, a good education, or finding the right partner in life are all wonderful things. But they'll all crumble eventually. I want to give my kids life abundant. Life eternal. This life actually is not a gift I can give them, it's only something God can give. I can introduce them to Jesus by passing on the gifts of grace he has given me. I can embody this forgiveness and grace in our lives together for eighteen years and beyond.

THE HEART OF JESUS

#BobLenz

I spoke a few years ago at a church in Pennsylvania that had recently hosted a junior high lock-in. Now, you know me, I love junior high students. I *still speak to them.* But even I admit, it is just a weird age. Zits are coming out of everywhere and they act as if they are powered by a six-pack of Red Bull.

One hundred junior high students attended this lock-in (an all-night youth event, which typically doesn't involve much sleep). They played games and worshiped into the wee hours of the morning. That night, one of the kids spilled a Coke, which stained the carpet. Later, a lock was broken when some students were racing to get to the front row in the sanctuary.

Oh, and fifteen people received Christ as their Lord and Savior.

But, because the church had to bring in a professional carpet cleaner and the lock had to be fixed, the elders of the church got together and voted that the junior high students could not have a lock-in at the church the next year.

It cost $35 to fix the lock. For the small price of a new

lock, a carpet cleaner, and a few tired adult volunteers, fifteen students found new life in Jesus. And a hundred students had the fact impressed upon them that there were adults in their community who cared about them.

If those kids were starving preschool students that lived on another continent, we probably wouldn't even think twice about writing that check. It would be the best money we had ever spent, and we would sleep well that night, patting ourselves on the back.

But when the students are pimply, loud tweeners in our own neighborhood, it's not as easy. But Jesus loves these kids. They are welcome in His Kingdom; they should be welcome in our churches.

The lock broke because teenagers were racing to *get into the church.* And the church elders voted to keep them out next time. If that's how we treat kids racing *to* the front of the church, why are we surprised that so many are walking the other way.

Sure, the lock needed to be fixed and the carpet needed to be cleaned. But this is what my friend Wes Roberts says:

> *"We don't want them to mess up, but when they do, there must be forgiveness, or else we do not believe in a God of redemption."*

If we can't offer forgiveness to rowdy teenagers, then we need to seriously reconsider the kind of forgiveness we think God offers to us.

I talk at schools across this continent about respect for elders and for property. I promise you: I will continue to do that. I teach kids the importance of respect, but with that said, I hope your church has the dirtiest carpet and the most broken doors of any church in your neighborhood. Youth matter to God; therefore they should matter to us too.

Let's look at another <18>. Matthew **18**.

> Matthew 18:5 says, "Whoever welcomes
> one such child in my name welcomes me."

Do you have a relationship with even just *one* child? One talkative neighbor kid that hangs around while you're trying to weed your front lawn? One part-time employee on the cash register who tends to show up late? One cereal-crunching toddler who sits behind you in church with his family? Or maybe one baby that cries in the wee hours of the morning, preventing you from getting sleep?

When we turn welcoming eyes to these little ones—who are, more often than not, inconvenient and messy—we turn welcoming eyes to Jesus. Youth and children are close to God's heart. If we want to be close to God's heart, we better get used to being around kids. When we dedicate ourselves to praying for and supporting the Next Generation, it is an evidence of our love for God. And since it's so close to God's heart, we might find that we actually enjoy it!

This is so close to God's heart, yet churches often don't allocate much of their budget towards children's ministry. Is it considered one of the less-important agenda items? Are we spending so much time entertaining adults, or maybe satisfying our own interests, that we're not fulfilling our mission of passing on the faith to the Next Generation?

But the good news is this: kids are *not* an agenda item. They're people, and there might even be a few of them living under your own roof.

> Matthew 18 continues, "If anyone causes one of these little ones—those who believe in me—to stumble, it would be better for them to have a large millstone hung around their neck and to be drowned in the depths of the sea."

Wow, that's a strong statement. Jesus cares deeply about this. This is close to the heart of God.

I ask you, as a part of the Body of Christ, how are you using your **talents, time, and treasures?** Are you sharing them with those close to Jesus' heart?

THE ENEMY IS TARGETING YOUTH

#BobLenz

Over the years, when I speak at schools, students will often come up and share an embarrassing moment with me. I was at a camp and a sixteen-year-old football player, Derek, came up and wanted to share his story.

Two weeks before he came to camp, he found out his parents were getting a divorce.

"I know it happens to a lot of people, but it still hurts. I just cried and cried. I had a friend who went through the same thing. He talked to me about it and that helped. I thought I was doing pretty good, until two days before I came to this camp.

"My dad came to me and said that the reason he was getting a divorce is that he found a new girlfriend. My dad said to me, 'I talked to your mom. She said she can handle the girls, your two sisters, but she doesn't think she can handle you.'"

Derek stood in front of me with his eyes diverted to the ground, "My dad looked at me and said, 'I just want to start a new life with my girlfriend, so we called social services. We are trying to get foster care for you until you are eighteen.'"

Derek looked at me and said, "Bob, do you know how embarrassing it is to tell your friends that your parents are in court because *neither* of them wants you?"

Too many of our youth are familiar with this kind of humiliating embarrassment.

I don't want to give the impression here that we are slamming divorced people. There is no condemnation in Christ. This is a book about hope and redemption, no matter what situation you might find yourself in. The divorce itself was not the reason that this young man felt unwanted by his parents. Even children whose parents are still married can get the impression by their parents' actions or words that they are unloved. No matter what situation you're in, please protect your kids, and don't use them as a weapon to get back at someone.

THIS IS A BOOK ABOUT HOPE AND REDEMPTION, NO MATTER WHAT SITUATION YOU MIGHT FIND YOURSELF IN.

Even if your parents are completely supportive and you have the kindest friends in the world, it is still difficult enough to be a teenager. Over the course of about a decade you may go from playing in a tree house to having your own second floor apartment. That's a lot of change for anyone. As a teenager, you may have the size and look of an adult, and may be treated like one long before you are proficient at maneuvering in the adult world. As if all of that wasn't hard enough, now kids are growing up in a time when photos and videos are posted online for the world to see in real time. There are now public and permanent visual records of things that, in previous generations, used to be private mistakes.

#RichMelheim

Childhood and adolescence is such a formative and vulnerable time. There are minefields and bombs in the lives of every youth and parent. Our children are being targeted from every direction. Media, advertisers, internet pornography, un-Christly messages, negative worldview and temptations — all of these threaten to shape and alter their future.

There are some things in this world that are obviously evil. I once stood at Auschwitz and peered into the inky blackness of the furnaces. I felt the sinister power of Evil. The world said, "Never again" after the Holocaust, but modern day atrocities and genocides happen every day. We speak of the evils of slavery as if they happened during the Civil War. Yet, around the world, children are still being kidnapped and sold into slavery and prostitution every day. There is more slavery in the world today than ever before. And persecution? I have friends in Pakistan who often text me to ask for prayer for their neighbors and children who are abused, raped and bombed because they are Christian. Every day Christians are targeted. After one Easter bombing at a church in Lahore, I received an urgent text telling me that children were in critical condition and in need of medicine, but the store owners would not sell it to them because they were Christian.

God's children being targeted is not a new thing. Do you remember the story of Israel prospering in Egypt? What did the Pharaoh do? He murdered the children.

When Jesus was born, the Magi who traveled from the east said to Herod, "We've traveled a long distance following the star. We have come to worship the king."

Herod said, "When you find him, tell me where he is, because I want to worship him too."

But did he really want to worship him? No. When the Magi didn't return, what did Herod do? He targeted the children. He killed every baby boy in the region under the age of two.

There was a god in the Old Testament named Molek. He was a small "g" god. He was described as having the body of a human and the head of a bull.

We certainly aren't foolish enough to worship something like that anymore. We would never try to trade securities under the symbol of a bull's head. (Well, except for Wall Street, I guess.) There is nothing wrong with Wall Street. Hey, I've got stocks for my retirement! I am not saying we should occupy. I just think we shouldn't bow down either.

It's easy for us to sit on our high horse and think that what we're doing is *not* bowing down. In ancient times they thought security came from a man-made object with a human body and a bull's head. Yet we tend to think our security comes from a man-made currency system. Think about how confident we feel when we log into our bank accounts or our retirement accounts and see our balance. Or conversely, how worried we are, depending on what it says.

Interestingly, Leviticus 18 is another <18> that gives us instructions for our children. Leviticus 18:21 says this:

> *"Do not give any of your children to be sacrificed to Molek, for you must not profane the name of your God."*

In that day, child sacrifices were required to please the ancient Molek. If a person wanted success, they wanted to make it, then they had to sacrifice their children.

People would come, put their babies on the altar, and the babies would roll down into the fire. The people could hear the babies scream and cry. They would play the drums louder and louder and faster and faster, so they wouldn't hear the cries of the children.

We might look back at that and wonder what monsters could turn their head away from hurting children?

Yet each day in our nation, there are an average of 5,240 suicide attempts by young people grades 7-12.[4]

And 17% of students in grades 9-12 have seriously considered suicide over the past 12 months.[5]

And we continue to beat our drums louder and louder and faster and faster. *I can't hear those kids. I don't know them. I have a lot of important things on my to-do list.*

We want more. Bigger. Faster. No matter what the cost. When we talk about "cost," it's easy to think only of the cost in dollars. Yet money is the cheapest of all of our resources. Money we can make; time we can't.

MONEY IS THE CHEAPEST OF ALL OF OUR RESOURCES. MONEY WE CAN MAKE; TIME WE CAN'T.

Is it possible that our lifestyle in this culture comes at a high cost to our children?

#BobLenz

We're not just pointing at the other people when we talk about this. Once my own daughter when she was younger said to me, "Daddy why do you like speaking more than you like being with us?"

What was I going to say?

"Because sometimes they clap! Last week at a school, I got a standing ovation! If just once you and your mom would stand up and applaud when I came home, then I would come here more!"

Of course I did not say that! But I had to stop and ask myself a tough question. Is that what my *actions* were saying? Was I sacrificing my family?

Our family has a little saying, "As a family we'll sacrifice, but we will never sacrifice our family."

Periodically, we need to reevaluate if our day-to-day

choices match our goal. Every other religion has to sacrifice to appease and please their god. Christianity is different. It's based on grace. It's not about being good enough, but what Christ has done for us.

Much of the evil in this world is blatant and unfit for the evening news, but the enemy is at work in much more subtle ways too. The enemy is called the *father of lies* in the scriptures. The lies told to our kids every day are enough to slowly take every ounce of fight out of them.

You're too fat.
No one loves you.
You only have value if you have a boyfriend,
and to get one you have to...
No one will get hurt.
It doesn't matter if you just cheat a little bit.
Don't ever go into public speaking.
Neither of your parents wants you.

It is certainly easy for us to buy into the lie that kids don't matter as much as adults do. Meanwhile, the enemy certainly knows the truth. He knows that these years are his best shot at knocking them out of the fight. He's targeting them every day. And his number one target is to destroy the faith of the next generation, to destroy their faith in God.

If we don't stand up for kids and empower them to stand, who will? If we don't give them truth to fight lies, who will? Know that the enemy will take the time. He will invest resources. He will do whatever it takes to target them.

Will we reach our youth? Will we have faith for the next generation?

IF WE DON'T STAND UP FOR KIDS AND EMPOWER THEM TO STAND, WHO WILL?

WHO, ME?

#yesyou #BobLenz

> "Therefore go and make disciples of all nations, baptizing them in the name of the Father and of the Son and of the Holy Spirit, and teaching them to obey everything I have commanded you. And surely I am with you always, to the very end of the age."
> —Matthew 28:19-20

Everybody seems to think it's a pastor's job or Billy Graham's job to share the good news, but it's actually something we are *all* called to do.

I was a youth director for seven years before I went full time on the road. One Friday night, I received a call from a student in my youth group. He said, "Bob! Bob! I have a friend over at my house, and I really think he wants to receive Christ. You have to come over!"

I responded, "That's awesome! I'm going to bed."

He said, "Bob, I don't think you heard me! My friend *wants to receive Christ.* You have to come over!"

I said, "I have already clocked sixty hours this week. I'm only a *part-time* youth pastor. I'm tired. I'm going to bed."

He said, "Pastor Bob, it's *your job!* You *have* to come over here."

Then I got mad; I already had the elders, the lead pastor, and the parents giving me my job description, and now a sixteen-year-old student was too!

So, I did something that *was* my job: I told him the word of God. "Ephesians 4:11-12 says, 'So Christ himself gave the apostles, the prophets, the evangelists, the pastors and teachers, to equip his people for works of service.' *That's* my job. My job is to equip you to do the work of God. So, if you don't know how to lead him to Christ, I didn't do my job. Good night!" And I hung up.

Then he was mad too! But that Sunday morning, he walked into the church with his friend, who was a new believer. He had led his friend to Christ. That's what it is about.

How many Christians never fulfill Jesus' last instructions, to go make disciples of all nations? Too many leave that job up to people like me.

When you read that verse in Matthew that says "Go and make disciples of all nations...," who do you imagine Jesus to be speaking to? The disciples, right?

Ah, the disciples. Those honored giants of the faith. Those learned men whose likenesses decorate stained glass, whose reflections shine down upon heads of states in large churches in important cities. Those heroes who authored New York Times Best Selling books such as *Matthew* and *Acts* and *1 Peter* and its thrilling sequel *2 Peter.*

Those are the people who are supposed to go into all the world and make disciples, clearly.

Not *me*.

How easy it is to think of the disciples that way, but the word "disciple" simply means student. They were not gods among men. The original disciples were more like trade school apprentices than seminary students. They were starting over midlife in a second career more than they were prodigies. They were loyal loudmouths and confused know-it-alls. Rather like junior high students, perhaps.

This command was just given to *people*—the only distinguishing category was that they were people following him. They were there looking at God. They were listening to God. To those who were following, watching and listening, he said, "Go into all the world and make disciples…"

So *everyone* is called to share the gospel.

The mental picture we have of an evangelist might be off the mark as well. You might think of an evangelist as a man in a suit who stands on a stage with a microphone in one hand and a Bible in the other.

SO *EVERYONE* IS CALLED TO SHARE THE GOSPEL.

A problem came in the 1980's; there was a spiritual gift analysis test that spread through many of the church bodies in North America. It was like a *StrengthsFinder* test, but for spiritual gifts. The creators of the test said that evangelism was one of the gifts, and I think that was a mistake.

Evangelism is not a gift. If it was, then it would be totally appropriate to say, "I don't have that gift. It's not my job."

According to Scripture, *the evangelist* is the gift.

Ephesians 4:11-12a says, "So Christ himself gave the apostles, the prophets, the evangelists, the pastors and teachers, to equip his people for works of service."

Therefore, *I'm* your gift. Me. Bob Lenz.

You may not *like* your gift. You may hope that God has a 90-day, no-receipt return policy. But like it or not, I am your gift. What is my responsibility as an evangelist? Not just to share Christ with those who don't know this loving God, but to call believers to daily return to the Author of Life, and to motivate us to share God's life with a weary world. My job is to equip us for the task of sharing Jesus.

So, what could happen if we really believed that it isn't the paid pastor's job to share Jesus, but that it is our job?

What could happen if we simply loved each other without strings attached, just as God loves us? What if we loved others, those not in the church? Our job is to sacrificially serve even the least important among us. Our job is to share the good news that God offers us reconciliation. God can fix the things we've broken in the world. God can fix the things that are broken in us. And God can fix the things that are broken by others.

That's *great* news.

Sharing that good news is our job. Not *my* job. *Our* job.

It's called the Great Commission, not the Great Suggestion.

We can't leave it up to the pastors. We can't leave it to the paid professionals. We must do our part. Will you join us? Will you share this good news with those around you and especially with those close to God's heart: the loyal loudmouths and confused know-it-alls, the students, the learners, the children?

We're talking about introducing God through our actions and words, almost as if we're tour guides walking through life, pointing out to our children the things of God in the world around us.

It's life-giving to show our kids a place we love. My wife and I have visited Hawaii a number of times on anniversary trips. On a recent trip, one of my daughters and her husband joined us. It made Hawaii come alive again for me, as I saw it through their wide eyes filled with wonder. I saw the waterfalls and the volcanoes, the beaches and the pork roasts with brand new eyes. I loved sharing that place of beauty with some of my beloved people.

This book is about sharing God with our kids in that way, like tour guides pointing out God. In fact, it's about bringing God into *all* the relationships in our lives because God's love is for everyone. Not just for *our* people, but for *all* people.

It is about seeing God in **structure** and in **spontaneity**. It's about meeting God in our **highs and lows**. It's about meeting God in our **hearts**, our **homes**, our **extended families**, our **friends**, our **church**, the **world**, and even meeting God in **eternity**.

Come, let us see what God has done.

PART 2.

What is the Good News?

WHAT IS THE GOOD NEWS?

#BobLenz

Have you ever encountered someone who wanted to share the Good News of the gospel with you, and then they spent a lot of time talking about the bad news? I wish they would at least open with this: "I've got good news and bad news. Which one do you want first?"

Personally, I would say, "Give me the good news first, please." Because on any given day, I'm already aware of a lot of bad news. Then I would just keep saying, "Oh yeah? Tell me more…" any time it seemed like they were ready to stop talking about the Good News.

Sometimes it might be appropriate to talk about the bad news with people. I think we've done a thorough job as a Christian culture of talking about the depravity of mankind, (something I do believe in), but it seems to me that we've missed the other side of the truth. We've missed the orthodoxy of dignity. We've missed the orthodoxy of the human value and worth.

Suppose you go to someone who has no context of God or the Bible and you say, "There is *nothing* good in you.

You need to be saved." It is possible that you will catch them at that exact moment when they realize that all of their goodness is never going to fix all of the mistakes they've made. But more often than not, you'll catch them squinting their eyes as they ponder your outrageous claim that there is *nothing* good in humankind. They might think:

"I've heard Jim Gaffigan. That dude is funny. Laughter is good. And...wait a minute! My daughter stood up for her younger brother on the playground last week! That was pretty good too. And I just spent all of this time thinking of how other people are good! So that probably means there is some kind of humble, good quality in me, too, darn it!"

I believe the law is written on our hearts. When you hear that, maybe you think that just refers to the guilty gut-feeling we have when we do something that we know hurts someone else. I definitely think that is part of God's law being written on our hearts. Even those who don't know God have an impression of a right and wrong that lines up impressively with the basic moral code of the Christian God: Don't kill. Don't take what isn't yours. Don't covet (coveting, or wishing you had what someone else has, will steal your joy and make you miserable. Any life coach could spend hours talking you through that one).

I think God's law being written in our hearts, though, is about much more than guilt. David in the Old Testament repeatedly says that God's Law brings *life*, and the Law is *good.*

I think that *good* gut-feeling we get when we are compelled to do something beautiful is *also* a result of God's law being written on our hearts. Love is the fulfillment of the law.

It feels good and right to love people because that's what we were made to do.

We are made for love.

We are made in the image of God. The reflection may be fuzzy, but most humans have at least caught glimpses of it. The loyalty of Grandmother's letters. The protection of an older brother. The gut-busting laughter of a kindergartener. Joy. Bravery. Humility. These are all reflections of the image of God.

WE ARE MADE FOR LOVE.

If you want to share the good news that Jesus paid the price for our sin, you might feel obligated to first share the bad news:

"While we were still ***sinners****, God saved us."*

Sin has been described as a lot of things. Missing the mark. Falling short. Turning in on oneself. A debt we can't pay. The Bad News. Yes. This is all true. This is the bad news we need to understand before we grasp the full meaning of God's forgiveness.

But there was good news that existed even *before* the bad news. Go further back than, "*While we were still sinners.*"

Back that truck all the way up to: "*In the beginning...*"

In the beginning, God said, *"It was good."* God's very first news about us wasn't bad news. It was good news.

It seems odd to me to be so upset about someone killing an embryo because it is made in the image of God—fearfully and wonderfully made—and yet at the same time be so adamant to explain to the grown up version of that embryo just how horrible a person they are. "You're a horrible person, but God loves you." If we step back for a second and try to hear that with fresh ears, it's possible to see how that would be confusing and hurtful.

Maybe we can try opening with the original good news, and following that up with the other good news.

Human brokenness and sin need to be a part of the conversation. It must have both law and gospel when we share the good news. And when we are talking about brokenness and sin, we should talk about our own more, and not theirs.

#RichMelheim

Jesus visited his hometown once and stood up in the synagogue to teach. The people were waiting on the edge of their seats to hear what he had to say. He opened up the scripture to Isaiah and read from it:

> "The spirit of the Lord is on me,
> because he has anointed me to proclaim good news to the poor.
> He has sent me to proclaim freedom for the prisoners
> and recovery of sight for the blind,
> to set the oppressed free,
> to proclaim the year of the Lord's favor."
> —Luke 4:18

Jesus said he came to bring Good News to the poor. If the church today was actually known for bringing good news to the poor, I think that would be considered Good News to this post-Christian world in which we live.

If we get back to being about what Jesus was about, that would be Good News that people need. It would be news they would actually hear. And it would be a mission the Next Generation would and could embrace.

Jesus declared that it was the year of the Lord, which was a celebration year when debts were forgiven and captives were set free in honor of the memory of God bringing them out of slavery in Egypt. If we, as God's people, declared freedom and forgiveness because of the work God has done in Jesus' death and resurrection—*that* would be Good News.

#BobLenz

When I talk about the good news, this is what I mean: that I am loved, valued, and forgiven by God.

God's love for us is good news for *you*, but it's good news for *me*, too.

I'll tell you why I think it's good news for me. When I was growing up, I thought that I wasn't worth very much. Whenever I speak about what it was like for me growing up, I don't usually tell everything. It would just be too much.

My dad hit his head when he was twelve. It was pretty serious, and after that he had epilepsy. Once, while we sat in the bleachers of the school gym to watch my brother play basketball, my dad had a seizure and it stopped the entire game. Everybody would turn around and look at us. Most people were nice enough and they wouldn't laugh, but they'd still stare at us with wide eyes and a look on their face that I could easily read: "What's wrong with *that* family?"

Two of my siblings were handicapped. Not because of genetics (I always want to say that so you don't think I'm handicapped too.) It was because of complications at birth. If they had been born via C-section they both would have been normal.

When my grandpa was 18, his arms were cut off while he was working in the mill. There's an <18> for you! He had two wooden arms after that. And I never saw my Grandma when she wasn't in a wheelchair. They lived next door to us. My mom cooked extra food every night and we brought it over to them. I had to go over after dinner and unbutton my grandpa's shirt for him, and put medicine on the corns on his feet because they couldn't do these things for each other.

Rich talks about how you get your meaning from the things surrounding you. Context gives meaning to words and symbols, and it also gives meaning to *us*. That describes my childhood exactly. I was surrounded by not one, but two handicapped siblings, a dad who stopped basketball games because of a head injury, and a grandpa with two wooden arms. Oh, and my older brother was a drug addict. As if I needed one more clue that something wasn't right with me either, I had a speech impediment and had a lot of trouble memorizing things at school. My context made it pretty clear to me that I wasn't worth very much.

Honestly—I *still* explain to people that it wasn't

genetic, whenever I mention my siblings. I joke about it, but I really don't want them to look at me and wonder if I'm handicapped too.

Because that is the picture that I have of myself. It is right there, ready to pop up at any moment. You know, it's that deeply engrained mental picture of yourself that you learn when you're a kid. That kind of thing sticks with you.

I have this vivid memory from when I was about ten of the police setting up a community event in a church parking lot. You could get a free license plate for your bike. A real metal one! We lived in a pretty small town. This was back in the day when there were only three channels on TV and cartoons were only on in the morning on Saturday, so pretty much all the kids under the age of puberty showed up. And a few gangly teenagers even stood in line sheepishly, pretending that they were only there to help their younger siblings.

I stood in line for hours to get my license. I'm not kidding you. Hours. As I neared the front of the line I heard one of the adults say that you had to know your address and phone number in order to get the license plate. I panicked.

I couldn't remember the numbers.

This was not just a momentary panic where your mind goes blank and then you laugh it off and the information comes back to you. I just *couldn't* remember things. I couldn't remember historical facts for quizzes. I couldn't remember multiplication tables. And I definitely couldn't remember my own address and phone number.

I stayed in line for a bit longer hoping the numbers

would somehow come to me in a vision from God, but they didn't. Before it was my turn, when there were just a few people in front of me, after waiting for hours, I quietly walked out of line and rode my unlicensed bike home.

I knew that my parents loved me, and I will always be so grateful for that, but I didn't know if I was worth loving. Value and love can be wrapped up together. And I wondered, even if I had *some* value in the world, did my brother and sister who were disabled?

I needed Good News. I needed to know that I was loved, valued, and forgiven.

The good news is that we are loved. Not hated. Not merely tolerated.

At first I had this picture in my head that God was constantly measuring my progress and was constantly disappointed. I knew that *I* was constantly disappointed in myself, and if I couldn't even meet my own standards, how could God possibly approve of me?

God does not stand at the pearly gates sighing heavily because of how much dirt we are tracking in on our boots. When Adam and Eve sinned for the very first time in the perfect garden, they sewed fig leaves to cover themselves and they hid from God. God did not wait for them to fix their own problems. God did not wait for them to clean up their mess, or even wait for them to beg for mercy. God came to be with them, just as He had always done.

God said, "Where are you?" Of course, *God* knew where they were. I can't claim to know what it is like to be omniscient, but I think I can get a tiny glimpse of just how little we see versus how much God sees, when I play hide and seek with my grandkids.

When my grandson Isaac was three, he ran just a few feet away from me, faced the corner and covered his eyes.

"Where are you?" I asked, smiling. "Where are you?" I played along with him. "There you are!"

I could see my grandson the whole time. I knew where he was. God knew where Adam and Eve were. *They* needed to know where they were.

God did not come at them yelling or glaring or sighing. Even in the consequences God laid out for humanity, grace was woven into every day. And a promise was given that a savior would be sent to set things right again. It's incredible to me that the very first prophecy about Jesus was given right after Adam and Even sinned for the first time. God didn't need a parent time-out, like I sometimes do, to cool down. Rather the *first* thought was to reconcile us to God and to each other. Because God doesn't hate us. Or just tolerate us. God loves us.

#RichMelheim

We are valued. We are valuable and have a purpose.

To most of the world, a person is only valuable if he or she is useful. Worth is determined by what we can produce. If we can't produce anything the world values - money, pleasure, or talented children, we are not considered worth much. In God's upside down economy, our value creates our purpose. Our worth is not based on what we do. It is based on the image in which we are created, and on the price God was willing to pay to redeem us.

God has made us valuable. Because we have this value, we also have a purpose: to bring glory and honor to God. Of course, God is already being glorified. Anywhere you look on this earth, creation reflects the glory of God.

I don't understand why we have allowed such tension between science and Christianity. Science textbooks are filled with praise songs that don't rhyme. The earth's core is believed to be as hot as the surface of the sun. Hard to imagine as you scrape ice off your sidewalks. The rocks are crying out praise. God *is already* being glorified. We get to participate in a unique way, because unlike the rocks and the trees and the earth's core, we are created in God's image and are relational. We get to love like God loves.

SCIENCE TEXTBOOKS ARE FILLED WITH PRAISE SONGS THAT DON'T RHYME.

A while back my favorite TV series was called *Parenthood*. It told the story of four generations of the Braverman family. The loyal but curmudgeonly Grandpa, the patriarch of the family, would often give advice to his grandkids when they faced difficulties. During one of these conversations, he'd often look them straight in the eye say, "Well, you're a Braverman!"

"You're a Braverman," is why they would be able to persevere during a difficulty, or why they should try to reconcile with a loved one. They were making the Braverman name known in the world. He was reminding them of what it means to be a Braverman. He was reminding them of what the name, and the children, should embody. He was not using it to shame them. He used it to call them forward to good things. To remind them that they will always be loved in his eyes.

One of the ways the Bible describes the relationship with those who love God, is to call those people God's children. As children, we carry God's name. We bring glory to God's name in the way we make that name known in the world.

I get to carry on the work of God in this world. The work of bringing good news to the poor, light into darkness, freedom to captives, and reconciliation.

#BobLenz

> "That God was reconciling the world to himself in Christ, not counting people's sins against them. And he has committed to us the message of reconciliation."
>
> —2 Corinthians 5:19

I saw something new in this verse recently, and I can't shake it. The first part of the verse and the last part are very familiar to me: *God was reconciling the world to himself in Christ....*

He has committed to us the message of reconciliation. These are basically the two things I spend my entire life talking about.

That small phrase in the middle, though, is what got me: *Not counting people's sins against them.*

That is how God reconciles people. God *doesn't* count people's sins against them. We are given the message of reconciliation, and therefore we also should not count people's sins against them.

But what are American Christians best known for? *Counting people's sins against them* might sum it up pretty well.

How in the world did that happen?

#RichMelheim

If the people who follow the most loving, sacrificial, welcoming person in history are thought of as hateful people, where in the world did we go wrong? Why did we let our narrative get defined like that?

If you're like me, you might think, "Yeah, but that public image Christians have is unfair. The loud, mean Christians get attention. There are so many who are following in the footsteps of Christ, just *doing* good and not making a fuss about it. They're not launching PR campaigns; they're just serving people."

That's a reality of the world we live in: bad PR is pervasive. It might be worth remembering that when you're reading a nice juicy news story about someone who holds a differing belief than you.

IF THE PEOPLE WHO FOLLOW THE MOST LOVING, SACRIFICIAL, WELCOMING PERSON IN HISTORY ARE THOUGHT OF AS HATEFUL PEOPLE, WHERE IN THE WORLD DID WE GO WRONG? WHY DID WE LET OUR NARRATIVE GET DEFINED LIKE THAT?

Yet, even so, I think we can take back our story. We don't have to let our story be told by others. We can tell it. We can name it. Claim it. And reframe it. We can name and claim for Jesus the acts of service we do.

We are often hesitant to connect our service with our faith. Service is *so* acceptable to the world. Faith is *so* not. But it is OK to give a plate of food in Jesus' name. It's interesting that people, and even entire religions who don't subscribe to everything Jesus, still hold him up as a good teacher. What is stopping *us*, the people who follow Jesus, from claiming Jesus' teachings as part of our heritage? Maybe if we stopped disconnecting our service from faith, faith would become more desirable.

You could say, "Here is a lunch bag with some granola bars, a toothbrush, toothpaste, a water bottle and some candy. I'm giving it to you in the name of Jesus. He's our guy. He was known for taking care of people, even people who were different from him, and even people who couldn't pay him back. We are God's children. We want to be known for what God was known for."

Or you can use your own words.

#BobLenz

We can also change the way our story is told by taking a moment to step back and really look at ourselves. Not look judgmentally at *those* Christians. Not blog about *9 Things the Church Is Doing Wrong These Days.* Instead I could just reflect on the one person whose actions I can control—me.

Is the defining mark of *my* life sacrifice and love? Or is my life marked by comfort? Is my aim to bring joy to others, or is my aim to seek joy for myself? Do I neatly contain the radical nature of Jesus' love into a bedazzling show on Sunday morning? Is it a wonder why that doesn't seem authentic?

Do *we* count people's sins against them?

I do.

Not counting people's sins against them is counterintuitive. It's not something we can accomplish through sheer effort. It comes through knowing *our* sins are not counted against *us*. We forgive because we are forgiven by God.

We are forgiven.

Often, we begin to understand forgiveness when we receive it from another person. That really fleshes it out, so to speak. It's like we can finally see it. Isn't it incredible that God has given us the chance to be the hands and feet of God's forgiveness to those around us?

God sent Jesus to live the perfect life on earth that we could not live. Jesus came to be the once-and-for-all sacrifice. Jesus took our sin upon himself on the cross. He was dead by the afternoon on Friday and buried in a tomb, a large stone rolled in front and Roman soldiers placed as guards.

But God raised him from the dead early Sunday morning. Then Jesus told his disciples to go spread the word: the curse of sin has been broken.

> *For God did not send his son into the world to condemn the world, but to save the world through him.*

That's John 3:17. The lesser known, younger brother of John 3:16. Just as good, but not as famous.

The good news is that God offers us eternal life. Not eternal waiting in the line at the DMV. Not eternal pain. Not eternal frustration. Not eternal to-do lists. Eternal *life*. Jesus describes this as *life to the full*. That's the kind of life I want. Life that is bursting at the seams. Life that overflows. Life that cannot be contained and cannot be stopped. Not even death can take away this kind of life.

We are given new, full life.

Sometimes the bad news in our life isn't our fault. I'm not saying we haven't done *anything* wrong. I'm saying that some people live in the reality that something done to them (abuse, rape), or things that can happen in the course of life on earth (cancer, mental illness), may dominate the landscape of their life.

If a predominant difficulty in your life is not even your fault, hearing "God forgives you" doesn't address the wound.

When we talk about sharing the good news with the Next Generation, let's remember that a big part of this good news is *life*. Jesus said, "I have come so that they might have life, and have it to the *full*." We believe and we have seen that God can restore broken hearts and trampled lives. We don't have easy answers for how this can happen. It may involve a lifetime of daily graces or daily choices. It may involve therapy. It may involve a safe and supportive community. Grief can be a long and winding road, but we have witnessed restoration in our own lives and in the lives of those we love. We don't have easy fixes, but we encourage you to stand with your people, your children, your friends, and your community when they encounter these difficulties. We can bring Good News by embodying the Good News of God: that we are loved, valued and forgiven by God. He offers us life that is full to the brim. That's good news for you, for me, and for everyone we know.

HOW CAN WE RESPOND TO THE GOOD NEWS?

#BobLenz

> *Love the Lord your God with all your heart and with all your soul and with all your mind and with all your strength.*
> — Mark 12:30

With all your heart.

God wants our hearts to be for him, just like his heart is for us. God wants our relationship to be wholehearted. It can't just be facts in our head. If love is real, it has to be from the heart.

When I was younger, my brother Bill told me that I was going to miss heaven by eighteen inches. I said, "God is a God of love, and if I got that close he would let me in." What I didn't understand was that he was talking about another 18 inches—from my head to my heart. So, let's talk about that <18> for a minute. My brother meant that I had information about God in my head, but I didn't know him and hadn't surrendered my life to him in faith.

What he meant was that all of this good news about God wanting friendship with me would stay in my head, and this life-changing news would never make its way to my heart.

For me this good news came into my heart when I was seventeen. I was a football player, and I was good enough to be a starter. I'd finally found a place where I fit—on a team. I felt respected. As a junior in high school I ended up going on a TEC weekend retreat (Teens Encounter Christ). The music wasn't at the professional level that we have at festivals today. It was actually just one guy with a guitar, singing with a big smile. And his smile was better than his performance. He started singing the song, *Father Abraham*, and he wanted all of us students to stand up and do actions while we sang.

I sat there, arms crossed. I didn't do the actions. That kind of thing was good for vacation bible school, but I was a starting lineman for the football team, for crying out loud.

But it was on this weekend that I met a pastor who said, "I've been a pastor for eighteen years, but I've only been an alive Christian for five."

And I asked, "What do you mean? How can you be a pastor and dedicate your whole life to this and not be an alive Christian?"

He said, "I had the information and theology in my head, but I didn't have a relationship of faith, and trusting, and surrendering my life to God from my heart. That's what it really needs to be: a heart connection."

So it was on that weekend that I realized that my

identity wasn't only about what I could accomplish by being a football player. My value and my worth didn't come from what I could do, but that I was loved unconditionally. I learned that God wanted me to be his child, and my identity came in knowing that. My faith became more than just religious activities. It became a faith relationship.

I didn't care anymore who saw me. I stood in the front row and sang the songs.

When we're talking about faith for the next generation, we want it to be from the core of who you are, from your heart. We want you to have a living relationship with the real God. We want you to be able to observe your own kids, to see when it's just a routine and to bring them to that point of a faith relationship that they own for themselves. We want to pass on faith that is not just a head-understanding, but a heart-relationship.

#RichMelheim

The human body is pretty incredible. You can anesthetize most of the human brain, and the heart keeps pumping. However if you anesthetize the heart, the patient quickly dies. We need to be *heart*quarters, not *head*quarters. When we talk about the heart here, we're talking about the core of who you are. The heart is a metaphor for compassion and love and tenderness.

In order to get to the heart of the problem we need to get to the problem of the heart. If our goal is to show someone God's love, that's not going to be accomplished through trying to prove there is absolute truth. Arguing isn't typically the best way to explain love.

YOU CAN ANESTHETIZE MOST OF THE HUMAN BRAIN, AND THE HEART KEEPS PUMPING. HOWEVER IF YOU ANESTHETIZE THE HEART, THE PATIENT QUICKLY DIES. WE NEED TO BE *HEART*QUARTERS, NOT *HEAD*QUARTERS.

Truth and heart are not enemies. Both are needed. We believe our God is more than just heart and love. We believe this God is truth. If someone is seeking the truth, we believe they will find God on that road. There are many great Christian thinkers who stand on that path, not just to hand out answers, but to ask questions of seekers, much as Jesus did.

There is an important place for apologetics, for discussing the truth. But what is the essence of that truth? The love of God in the person of Jesus Christ. Scripture is revealed truth. To love God, our hearts must encounter truth in scripture and in the person of Jesus.

What do we know about God? About truth? About love? There is much mystery. All the books in the world could never explain everything, but the clearest revelation of what love and truth are and who God is can be found in the person of Jesus Christ. So if we can set up an experience of the heart—to experience that Jesus, to experience the one who calls himself that truth, the one who is truth *and* love—that's what our kids need. That's what our hearts long for. That's what we were designed for. That's the vision and that's what we want for the Next Generation.

So, let's get back to the basics: the Word and the Word made flesh, the Bible and the person of Jesus. Let's go back and look at the earliest days of Christianity. The Greeks in that day were great arguers and great philosophers. They could prove that a circle was square. No one could out-philosophize the Greeks. When they looked at the cross, it was folly. The weak god who died on a cross and couldn't even save himself was a joke. That was not a god worth following. A god worth following would have been a god who was a winner, then destroyed the other cultures.

In the early days of Christianity, the cross was a joke to the Greeks and a stumbling block to the Jews. It was an insult, a scandal. Anyone hanging on a tree is cursed. *No,* they thought, *God doesn't operate this way.*

So how did Christianity ever spread across the world? It spread through the people who *met* Jesus. These were the people who had known the risen Christ. They had been fed by Jesus when they were hungry, and healed by him. They had been forgiven and experienced the way Jesus loved without strings. In that context, the message of the cross begins to make sense. The folly of a sacrificial God begins to make sense.

The world we live in has a lot in common with the first century. Today we have great minds who are great arguers.

And great arguers who don't even have great minds. The thinkers and the debaters of our time will not be wooed by mere argument alone.

We also have the deeply devout religious crowd, and a message of free grace from God is still a stumbling block. *Good deeds count for nothing? God's reconciliation is available to all?*

The people who met Jesus in the first century shared his message in the same way they came to know him. Through word and deed. Through their lives. They loved as Christ loved.

You can't argue love. You can argue philosophy until you're blue in the face and blue in the faith, but you can't argue love.

We believe that Christianity will hold up to discussion and debate, but that is not going to win hearts. It is not an argument that is going to convince your kid or your friend. The argument that is not an argument is what wins. Love wins.

We believe that faith in God is rational but we're not going to argue about it. Facts and ideas can be expressed and stated, but then we need to do what Jesus did and love. We need to address the heart, in the language of the heart: love.

We need to go back to the future. We need to "heart" people like they did in the first century. We need to go back further than the most recent chapter of American Christianity, and further than the Reformation. In those times, Christians were correcting theological courses. They were explaining God more accurately to people who already knew God. In our time, most people do not know God. Our post-Christian world has a lot in common with the pre-Christian world of the first century.

At the heart of the matter is not our love, but Jesus' love. We love because he first loved us. First, the heart of the matter is the matter of the heart. But there's more. Jesus said we are to love God with all our minds, too.

With all your mind.

#RichMelheim

> **THERE ARE <18> INCHES FROM THE HEAD TO THE HEART. BUT THERE ARE ALSO EIGHTEEN INCHES THE OTHER DIRECTION: FROM THE HEART TO THE HEAD. THAT IS AN IMPORTANT <18> TOO.**

There are <18> inches from the head to the heart. But there are also eighteen inches the other direction: from the heart to the head. That is an important <18> too.

We should stop thinking about our minds as weapons to wield against others and refocus that energy on using them as a tool for serving God and his people. We're not going to argue anyone into loving God. Yet what a loss it would be to abandon the brain, instead of using it to love and serve the Lord.

What could it look like to love the Lord with all your mind? What if those gifted with organizational problem-solving, or engineering creativity, or teaching skills used those gifts for the betterment of humankind? Using our brains is a way to love God with our mind by loving those around us.

When you're born you have a one-pound brain. By the time you're an adult you have about a three pound brain. At age sixteen you actually have about 15% more brain than your parent. There is this blossoming of neurons. You just don't have all the connections. Teenagers have all of the equipment of an adult body. But they lack the adult judgment center. They may look like an adult. They may want to be treated like an adult. Society tells them to shout out: "Treat me like an adult." The problem is, they simply aren't. They lack the connected adult brain - the prefrontal cortex. They won't have it until - get this - the same year as their car insurance rates go down: about 25.

You actually go through six different major times in your life when the brain adds billions of neurons. Then the growth plateaus out for a few months or years while it hooks them together. Billions of more neurons are added again, then your brain hooks them together again and prunes out those that aren't being used. These times parallel pretty closely to the typical tension points in parenting. The *Terrible Twos*, for example, is a time when little ones are adding a whole bunch of things and don't know what to do with them. The child is just testing things, trying to make connections. *Does this work? What about this?*

I know enough about neurology to understand that what you put in at the beginning is there at the end. You want to put God's Word indelibly in the place where you are going to make all of your decisions in life. Fix God's Word in your head.

When we put pathways in place that bring us to the throne of grace, we love God with our minds.

#BobLenz

One of the reasons I wanted to write this book with Rich is his understanding of, and respect for, scripture. Everything is drawn back to the Word of God when you talk to Rich.

When we sat together and talked about what it means to each of us to share the gospel, Rich always led us back into the Word.

Rich has a passion for instilling this Word of God into the hearts of young people. It comes from his understanding of neurology and also from his personal experiences growing up immersed in faith traditions of a mainline denomination. These traditions were not empty for him. They were modeled to him in authenticity and taught by people who were living out these ideas in their daily lives.

I know many people who have grown up in mainline denominations and have found certain rituals or traditions to be void of life and grace. I deeply appreciate the real wound that leaves. It can leave a bad taste in our mouth for anything that smacks of repetition.

Rituals don't have to be void of life. If you want to grow

tomatoes, repeated watering will bear more life than sporadic or one-time watering. Habit and repetition can bear fruit.

Rich's parents lived in a way that mirrored their words. The Lord's Prayer was recited every Sunday, and the ideas were lived out in their lives. On Thanksgiving, his family set up folding chairs and borrowed card tables from church, so they'd have enough room at the table to welcome anyone who might otherwise be alone. In any given year, they'd have an assortment of people from their community—maybe college students who couldn't afford to travel back home over break, or recently widowed members of their church. In that house, the memorized prayers and scriptures were lived out.

His mom would say, "How could you call yourself a Christian and leave those people alone on what might be the loneliest day of the year for them?"

My parents lived it out too. My mom had the same philosophy as Rich's mom. Our table was regularly filled with friends and strangers, as my parents lived out the words of Jesus. Carol and I carried on that tradition in our home. Now our kids live that way too, in their own homes.

Now that my kids are grown, I look back at how we spent our time together, and there is much that I'm proud of: we passed on that tradition of hospitality, and we made a habit of spending time every night talking about our highs and lows together and praying together and discussing God's Word. We modeled this love in our house. We taught our kids a lot about God's love and God's Word, but one thing that I do wish is that I had given them more scripture in those years when their brains were learning sponges.

My daughter went to a Bible college and after the first semester, she said to me, "Dad, I wish I knew more Bible verses. It's so hard to memorize them now." My Joyel is such a bright light in this world. She loves with the love of Jesus, deeply and exuberantly. But during those early years where it is easiest for our brains to learn, kids aren't yet old enough to decide for themselves, "What do I want to learn now, while it's easiest for me to learn?" A musical instrument? Another language? A sport? Scripture? It's still *our* job as parents to decide what is worth their time. We make sure they brush their teeth. We make sure they do their homework. What else do we want to give them?

I made sure that my kids knew I loved them. I made sure they knew God's love. But I do wish I'd given them the chance to learn more scripture during this critical time. That's one of the reasons I love what Rich does. He loves the Lord with all his mind.

He has hundreds of Bible verses set to music. Learning scripture through music is a great whole brain, whole body way to learn it. There are links to many of these songs in the Appendix of this book.

With all your Strength.

#RichMelheim

If we think about our mind being centered in our brains, and we think about love being centered in our hearts, then try thinking about strength like it's centered in your hands. It's what you physically *do*.

Maybe when we hear "With all your strength," the picture that pops in our mind is that emoji of a bicep flexing. Or maybe wrestling suits and sweat and grunting. That is *one* kind of strength.

But what is *our* strength? What do we do in this world?

If we're gifted in music, that's a strength! If we are a leader, that's a strength! If we love to plan events, that's a strength! God has given humankind a variety of gifts. It is a form of worship to use these gifts for betterment of people and advancement of God's kingdom.

Whatever our strength is, let us love God with all our strength. Not a little bit of it. Not whatever is convenient. We should put our backs into it. Use some elbow grease. Love the Lord with all our elbow grease.

We can love God with the talents that come easily. We can love God with the weaknesses that turn into strengths. We can love God with weaknesses that we struggle with our entire lives. All of our strength, as weak or strong as it is.

Jesus tells us to love God not only in our hearts (in emotion and in love), and not only in our heads (in our ideas and plans), but also in our strength (what we do in the world).

I love that Jesus doesn't just want our relationship with him to be in an invisible, spiritual realm. Jesus continually shows that he cares for our physical, daily lives. One-third of Jesus' ministry was healing. He decidedly cared for people's physical body. Taking care of people's physical needs is a great way to share the good news of God's love.

WE CAN LOVE GOD WITH THE TALENTS THAT COME EASILY. WE CAN LOVE GOD WITH THE WEAKNESSES THAT TURN INTO STRENGTHS.

If you've ever been involved in the care of another human—whether it's a baby, an aging parent, or professionally in child care or healthcare—you know just how personal it can be. This care can be an act of serving God, and even a way to share God's love.

With all your Soul.

#Rich Melheim

There are a couple of ways to think about what the soul is. In the original Hebrew, the word *soul* meant all of you, the tangible and the intangible. Whatever it is that makes you, you. Your soul includes feelings that come up unbidden—sadness, anger, laughter. It also includes things you decide to do. Your will, you could say.

Your soul is *you*.

I grew up unaware of my dyslexia. From the time I was able to pick up a pencil, I began drawing pictures to help me remember things. It wasn't until I was in my 50s and I started researching learning disabilities in order to build www.richlearning.com into an optimal preschool learning environment that I discovered my "disability." I remembered I had to go to "special class" to learn to read. If you ever see me at a conference, you'll likely see me drawing there. It's one of my strengths, though I guess it came out of something people might call a weakness. Strengths are funny that way.

So when I think about what the soul is, a list of words isn't as helpful to me as a picture. Let's think about the soul like the soles of your feet. The weight of you—all of you—rests on the soles of your feet. The soul can also be thought of as the will. That's like our feet too. They move us in the direction we choose to go.

What are your intentions, and how can you use them to love God? Where will you go?

#Bob Lenz

Your soles make impressions on the world where you stand. What impression do you want your *soul* to make on this world?

How can the imprint you make in this world be a way that you love God? It looks different for each of us, but no matter what your presence is in the world, think about being tasteful. I don't mean be reserved or inoffensive. I mean, be *full* of taste. Think about being tasty, leaving an impression that leaves people wanting more of what you have, instead of leaving people with the feeling of being glad you're gone.

Let's make sure we're sharing the good news with a good taste, a good impression.

YOUR SOLES MAKE IMPRESSIONS ON THE WORLD WHERE YOU STAND. WHAT IMPRESSION DO YOU WANT YOUR *SOUL* TO MAKE ON THIS WORLD?

And Love Your Neighbor As Yourself.

#RichMelheim

We started this section by looking at this verse in Mark 12:29-30

> "The most important [commandment]," answered Jesus, "is this: Hear, O Israel: The Lord our God, the Lord is one. Love the Lord your God with all your **heart** and with all your **soul** and with all your **mind** and with all your **strength**."

Now let's look at the next verse, Mark 12:31:

> "The second [greatest commandment] is this: '**Love your neighbor as yourself.**'"

Some people have the impression that the golden rule was something Jesus came up with right there. But do you see those little quotation marks? He was quoting scripture.

"Love your neighbor as yourself," is actually one of the Old Testament laws in Deuteronomy.

Since the very first time God gave us instructions for living together, caring for each other has always been part of the plan. When Jesus came and shook things up, this isn't something he changed. Rather, it was something he underlined. He repeated to his followers these kinds of directives:

> *"Whatever you do to the least of these, you do to me."*
>
> *"If you love me, love your brother."*
>
> *"Whoever says he loves me, but hates his brother, does not have the love of God in him."*

These things are only possible through the gospel. We can't do them in our human strength. I get fired up about wanting to make a difference in this world. Bob gets pretty fired up too. He often has to wipe away tears during his stories. They are genuine tears pouring out from his heart. With passion like that, it could be easy to see the injustice or hurt in the world and be immobilized by it. Bob & I travel across the world to slums and we speak in front of tens of thousands of leaders at conferences. We want to see change happen on a global scale. We want *mountains* to move. We want *everyone* to hear about God's love for them.

The way we will move mountains is to start right where we are at with our piece of it. There isn't one thing that's bigger than the other when it's done in the name of the Lord for the purpose of caring for the people God created and loves.

These directives Jesus gave are on a very small and personal scale. The world starts right here, with us, in our home, with our kids, our brothers, our sisters, our neighbors.

THE WORLD STARTS RIGHT HERE, WITH US, IN OUR HOME, WITH OUR KIDS, OUR BROTHERS, OUR SISTERS, OUR NEIGHBORS.

Our greatest life's work awaits. Let us be a conduit of God's love and grace to our children, brothers, sisters, neighbors, and strangers.

So let's think long term. Let's think eternal. The real stages for sharing this are the smudgy kitchen benches and the wobbly coffee shop bistro tables, the bedside at night and the morning commute to school. So, stick a bunch of folded napkins under that wobbling coffee shop table, and let's get started.

GOOD NEWS WANTS TO BE SHARED

#BobLenz

Good news is something that can't be contained. We even use social media to share our good news:

Laura won student of the month! Italy is beautiful! We found the perfect sledding hill! U2 puts on the best concert, like, ever! I made meatloaf from scratch and it wasn't gross! I got that promotion!

It's not enough to high-five yourself. We are compelled to update our status, to tweet, to Instagram. We must proclaim this amazing news around the kitchen table, in our cul-de-sac, and on the World Wide Web. Or "in Jerusalem, in all Judea and Samaria, and the ends of the earth," so to speak. That's how Good News works. It cannot be contained. It must be shared.

Our prayer for you is that you may know the peace that comes from being loved, known, and forgiven by God, and that you may know the joy it is to share that peace with those you love.

My daughter, Amber, gave birth to her first baby at

6:30 AM after being in labor for 24 hours. We were at the hospital by 7:15 AM and my daughter pulled me close to her and pleaded, "Dad, you can't tell anyone yet. I am *so tired.* I have to get some sleep. Don't tell anyone until noon. Just give me that long."

"You want me to wait?!" I could hardly process her request.

"Dad, you know that as soon as you tell people, everyone will call and text and visit, and I won't be able to sleep!"

"But, who *can* I tell?" I was really trying.

"No one, Dad. Please, give me until noon," she said.

I promised I wouldn't put it on the internet like I did when my daughter, Danielle, had her son, but Amber agreed to let me tell some of my friends out in California. I swore them to secrecy.

THAT'S HOW SHARING THE GOSPEL COULD BE. IT COULD BE SHARED LIKE GOOD NEWS, BURSTING FROM OUR MOUTHS.

I couldn't *not* tell anyone. This was the greatest news!

That's how sharing the gospel could be. It could be shared like good news, bursting from our mouths.

I have heard that most Christians haven't led anyone else to Christ. That means most Christians haven't fulfilled the Great Commission. But just imagine what could happen if you started sharing the good news like it's something so exciting you just can't keep it in. What if we shared it with one person the way we share news about new babies, or new jobs, or our children's successes.

What if we lived out our faith in front of one person, sharing God's love in action in our life and sharing the reality of Christ in our words, because faith comes by hearing the Word of God? Say we shared our highs and the lows, that's real life, and brought them to God, that's called prayer. We could look together to God's instruction book and love letter, which is the Word of God. Maybe we could sing worship prayers together and gather together, which is called church. All of this together is called discipleship.

Say we just tried to do this for six months or so. That's not that big of a commitment. It is less than a school year. It's the length of one football season. On the other hand, it is rather a long time. It takes the weight off of one single conversation. It's long enough that we're not talking about one intense conversation. We're talking about the good news, love in action and in word, shared in the context of your real life and her real life.

If we all did this, no one person would have to have the weight of telling the whole world, but all of us, all over the world, would participate in the joy of getting to share God's love with the people in our corner of the world.

What if we didn't grumble, "Who do we *have* to tell?" Instead we asked, "Who do we *get* to tell?" We could say, "Hey, have you heard…? Did you hear…?" We can't hold it in anymore.

PART 3:

<18> Faith Experiences To Have With Your Kids Before Age <18>

OVERVIEW OF THE <18> EXPERIENCES.

Plan Your Work and Work Your Plan.

#RichMelheim

What would it look like if we put as much thought into our children's spiritual development as we put into planning our summer vacation?

"Plan your work and work your plan," my Grandma used to say.

WHAT WOULD IT LOOK LIKE IF WE PUT AS MUCH THOUGHT INTO OUR CHILDREN'S SPIRITUAL DEVELOPMENT AS WE PUT INTO PLANNING OUR SUMMER VACATION?

We have the opportunity to spend <18> years investing in the spiritual development of our kids. We have the chance to take that as seriously as we take their educational development, their character development, and their physical development.

Any plan we have for parenting will have to be a flexible plan because a lot of things change over the course of <18> years. The way we relate to our kids varies from year to year and from family to family, depending on age, culture, family situation, parenting styles, parent and child personalities, and our family histories. The <18> principles listed here are designed to be modified to fit your unique situation. Some are disciplines or postures to be assumed on a daily or weekly basis. Some are one-time events.

These are <18> of the best things you can do with your kids. We have purposefully listed things for you to do *with* your child. They are not *<18> things we should teach our kid about God before it's too late*, or even *<18> signs of a healthy young adult*. They are simply <18> experiences that we found to be life-altering for us and for our kids. These are the things that have brought us into a relationship with God. We chose experiences backed up by research and the experiences of others. We have tried to include a variety of examples.

We have intentionally included experiences that encompass more than just you and your kids in your own home. They cover seven different arenas: Your **heart**, your **home, cross+generational relationships**, **friendships**, the **local church congregation**, out in the **world**, and through **eternity**. Some experiences are firmly planted in one arena or another; many of them overlap into multiple arenas. It's important to think about how the Good News is relevant to each one.

Our Hearts.

When we think about who needs the Good News, we must not forget our own need for God, our own need for the Good News.

We need to hear it *once* and *daily*. We need to hear it for the first time and then hear it again and again. We want to take a moment here and talk about this idea because we know many people who have come to a point in their life when they sincerely received God's forgiveness, but they find that they still sin. They want to live wholly holy but they feel like they are just as much of a sinner as ever, and the solution is to get re-saved or to do a recommitment. There can be appropriate times for a recommitment, but I think some of the angst can be calmed by simply understanding that we are sinner and saint at the same time.

I'm right in God's sight because God sees Christ in me. I am a beloved child of God. I am a saint. Yet, until the day of my resurrection, I will still remain a sinner here on earth. We live in this tension.

Does that mean we never mature? Not at all.

Here's another way to look at it: I am saved, I am being saved and I will be saved.

I am saved from the penalty of sin. I am saved from damnation, or separation from God. This salvation happened once at the moment you received his grace, when Christ offered his life in exchange for yours. I am saved. Past tense. "It is finished," as Jesus on the cross proclaimed.

I am being saved, in the present, from the power of sin. That's where discipleship comes in. That is the transformation of my old self into a new creation. The Reformer Martin Luther wrote in his Small Catechism: "The sinful self with all its evil deeds and desires must be drowned through daily repentance." As I surrender daily, the Holy Spirit renews and redeems me. Present tense. Current. Daily. I grow and want to keep growing in faith.

Finally, **I will be saved** in the future. One day after I draw my last breath on earth, I believe in the power of Christ I will again rise. I will be saved from the very presence of sin and will be with God forever. I will be welcomed into God's presence and there will be neither sorrow nor pain.

I am saved, I am being saved, and I will be saved. If our greatest need was simply for wisdom, God would have sent us a teacher. If our greatest need was for justice, God would have sent a prophet. If our greatest need was for food or progress, God would have sent an agronomist or engineer. But our greatest need was and is still for something much more profound and powerful. Our need was, is, and always will be for a remedy for sin. So God sent a savior. Or rather, God came as a savior to do for me what I could not do for myself.

Our Homes.

We are the shepherds of our own homes. Our kids' spiritual growth is our responsibility, not our pastors'. As parents, we have the privilege of shaping our children's lives. How often will they floss? What are their bedtimes? Do they learn a sport or an instrument?

Spiritual formation is no different and is shaped in large part by the parents. What Bible stories are familiar? What do we take to God in prayer? What do we learn about what work God has done in our own family history?

It's not a question of *if* we'll teach our children. The question is *what* are we teaching them?

Ailyce and I went through infertility, multiple surgeries and treatments for five years. We said, "God, maybe your will for us is to take care of the kids in the youth group." We were set up for adoption when Catherine Elizabeth, and then three years and another surgery later, Joseph Martin, were born. Finally, we got to hold a baby in our arms.

If God has put someone on our heart and into our world, then we should care for them, whether a child in our home or a youth group at church. We should do as Jesus says: "Feed my lambs and feed my sheep." Paul, speaking by the Holy Spirit, said, "Tend my flock of God that is in your charge."

What flock are you in charge of?

Whether the flock in your charge is a baby, grandma in a nursing home, or a youth group at your church, they are all flocks of God. Maybe they aren't the ones you wanted, but they are God's. God wants them. And God asks you to feed them and care for them.

Cross+generational Relationships.

Our culture has become increasingly segmented by age. From the earliest days of daycare, we are often sequestered into little micro-communities of people no more than eleven months away from our own age. Two-year-old preschool is separated from Three-year-old preschool, and this continues through high school. In adulthood our age range broadens a bit, but we're still likely to maintain most of our relationships with people who are like us—young adults, or families with young children, or empty-nesters.

In this fragmented world, we have almost lost one of the most beautiful gifts God has given humans: cross+generational relationships. Every generation has needs and gifts. We think of babies, for example, as having lots of needs. And they certainly do. They require a lot of hands-on care and patience. They also have a unique gift, as any caregiver can attest, of being able to bring you into the present moment. They have a gift of helping us leave the worries behind. They have this amazing gift of helping us rediscover the wonder of the world.

The elderly have needs, but also immense gifts of wisdom and insight, and often they have gifts of time.

I was at a youth gathering recently and one of the young women told me that their church always packs their own food when they go on these weekend retreats. She said the youth plan and pack the meals, but all the old ladies in the church load them up with treats. They send cookies, Rice Krispie bars and ice-cream-buckets full of puppy chow and trail mix. Then the teenagers take pictures of themselves eating the snacks, and they write thank you letters to these women.

What great gifts these generations are giving to each other.

With Our Friends.

We go places our pastor does not go. We may sit at a desk in a cubical. Or have coffee after dropping off the kids at school. We may sit on the PTA board. We may be the assistant coach for the youth soccer team.

We can bring the light of Christ wherever we go. With our friends, our neighbors, and our co-workers.

In Our Church.

Two of my favorite people in the world are in their twenties and they have these wonderful hearts. They're my kids. My daughter is thinking of doing a double masters in theology and social work. Whether she ever goes to a church or not, she will be a church. She is the embodiment of Jesus in the world where she lives.

If we are people who love going to church then it makes sense that we want that for our kids. We want them to find a church they will love. There is so much good a local congregation can offer that can't be found anywhere else in our culture.

Is the "church" we want for our kids inside the building walls for ninety minutes on a Sunday morning? If 98% of our mission is *outside* the doors, and most of our churches spend 98% of the time *inside* the doors, there's something screwy there. It certainly isn't appealing to a young person who wants to change the world.

One of the things I regret most as a father is talking too much and listening too little. What if we listen to these vibrant young hearts? I think we're fighting a losing battle if we're desperately begging the next generation to come stay with us inside a church building, instead of raising them to be the church wherever they are.

We could *be* the church with them in our homes, in our passions and in their passions. Instead of only asking them to bring their friends to church, we could encourage them to bring church to their friends.

What if we considered that only a small part of our mission happens on Sunday morning? What if only a small part of our resources were devoted to those few hours?

I think the church where we meet together once a week in a local congregation shouldn't hold more importance than the church we *are* in our homes, our work, and our lives the rest of the week.

Having said that, the time we have together, meeting as a local congregation, is a unique opportunity to give and receive Jesus. Let us not forget about the beautiful opportunity to embody God's love to our neighbors within our church walls. They may have come to this holy huddle in order to meet Jesus, and they can meet Jesus in *us.*

Even in church, let's not expect the pastor to be our *only* conduit of God's Word. That's the old system. In the Old Testament, priests were the connection point between God and people. Only the High Priest could enter the special room covered with a thick curtain—the Holy of Holies. This was a visceral picture that God was holy. God was holy and not to be taken lightly. But something happened on the night that Jesus died on the cross. Across town in the Holy of Holies in the temple, that thick curtain mysteriously ripped from top to bottom, signifying that God had come to be among us. Jesus' death on the cross was a one-time good-for-all redemption that means we can have access to God anytime, anywhere. Forty days later, God sent the Holy Spirit to the believers, and a new system was instituted. We don't have to *GO* to church to find God. Now, God lives in us.

When we go to church, hopefully we are fed by the sermon, the songs and prayers. But we can also be fed by the family sitting next to us in the pew. And, in turn, they can meet Jesus in our words, our kindness, or our listening ear.

Likely on any Sunday morning, part of our local congregation will be bursting with good news, and others will be barely holding it together with grief. We worship God in the sanctuary, but we also worship God when we listen to each other in the foyer.

Church is a place to meet with God. Though many have rightly noted that now God lives in us and we can meet with him anywhere—field, forest, or beach. Church is still an important place to meet with God's people, young and old, those we know well and those who are strangers, those like us and those quite different.

In The World.

We are to follow Jesus' example and care not just for our own parents and brothers and sisters, not just for our own church family, or our own friends. Jesus took time for strangers on the side of the road and even for crowds so dense that they prevented him from getting where he was trying to go. What if we, in the crowded subway train or on a crowded freeway, looked at each moment as an opportunity to treat someone with dignity? To love as God loves, instead of looking at them as objects that are in our way?

Sharing the Good News in the world is a responsibility that is given to each one of us, not just the evangelists like Bob Lenz.

God is in the world already—all of creation is held together in Jesus. We are to be like tour guides, pointing God out.

In The Church Eternal.

We don't share The Good News with the eternal church, with those who have gone before us. Rather, *they still share with us*. Elijah, Esther, Calvin, Dr. Martin Luther King Jr., and our own personal ancestors have all tread this trail before us. There is much encouragement and insight we can receive by remembering those who have gone on before. Though we hope your loved ones don't have to deal with mourning a death early in their life, we have the comfort of knowing we will be reunited in God's restored kingdom, where all our tears will be wiped away.

1. <18> MINUTES EVERY NIGHT

#RichMelheim

Talk about it when you walk on the way,
when you lie down, and when you rise.
—Deuteronomy 6:7 (paraphrased)

When I was a kid my Mom would read a chapter or two from a book, and then she shared scripture with us. Sometimes she would tell us a story from the Bible, like Samuel growing up in the temple, and sometimes she would share a short verse or a proverb. After that we would pray together. We listened to her every night as she prayed for us, and as she brought her own joys, as well as her requests and worries, to God.

As a child, I enjoyed that time immensely, but I didn't think much about it as I grew older. I used to dislike rituals, in fact. I wanted to do new things instead of repeat the same old things. I wanted to pass on faith to youth in a way that highlighted all of the excitement. Nothing old. Only new!

The more I learned, though, the more it became clear to me that these habits and routines are the things that create a firm foundation in a way that one-time experiences couldn't match. The things we do over and over again are the things that shape us. In my formative years, I went to bed every night hearing that God loves me, my parents love me, and watching my mom and dad take their highs and lows to God in prayer.

There is some interesting science about how influential those final moments before bedtime can be. Let's start by looking at cortisol, the primary stress hormone. Cortisol blocks melatonin, the sleep hormone. So being stressed at night can prevent us from getting a good night's sleep.

Just hearing that fact makes my cortisol levels spike! Great! Now when I lay down at night to sleep and a worrisome thought pops into my brain, I can *add to it* the fact that stress makes sleep more difficult! *That'll help me sleep.*

A brain restores itself during sleep. Getting enough sleep helps with creativity and innovation. If boys don't develop healthy sleep patterns as a child, they are three times more likely to have clinical depression, and girls are five times more likely. A child's brain cells grow at night, so if there's too much stress and not enough sleep, those cells get eaten up and are gone for over. An adult's sleep is important too. After age forty I start to lose about ten thousand neurons each night.

I'm already hyperventilating. Anyone else? I don't have that many neurons to lose, do I?

Unfortunately, if you live on earth, stress is not going to be completely avoidable. If you have a baby at home, you're probably not getting enough sleep. If you have teenagers, you're also probably losing sleep! If you live a relatively comfortable upper-middle class life, then your family likely feels the strain at school and work to "make the grade." Perhaps your afternoons, evenings, and weekends are filled with activities. It doesn't take much to get stressed out about getting everything done on time.

If you live with limited resources, you have a very real stress of financial or food insecurity. If you are able to live completely off the grid without the stress of social media and cell phone pings, then your stress might be about the lack of rain or the infestation of potato bugs. We can limit stress in our lives, but we cannot eliminate it. There is no magic place on earth without stress.

THE MERE IDEA OF REDUCING STRESS IS STRESSFUL.

Right on schedule, according to my family history, I had a severe heart blockage at age fifty. When I woke up from the surgery, my wife, Arlyce, stood next to me and said, "The doctor said you need to change three things in your life: diet, exercise, and stress."

I was hooked up to all of the after-surgery tubes, but I still managed to yell into the hallway, "Come on, I have teenagers! Tell the doctor two out of three ain't bad!" I could manage my diet and exercise easily enough, but how could I possibly get rid of stress? The rate of the heart monitor beeping increased for the next few minutes as I pondered how to reduce stress in my life.

The mere idea of reducing stress is stressful.

Many books and articles have been written about managing stress. Interestingly, many of them mirror Christian values. You can manage stress through meditation, serving others, and having a support system, and even by having a moral compass which helps inform your decisions.

There is one important thing we can do to help with stress at nighttime. We can talk about God's Word when we *lie down*, as Deuteronomy 6 prescribes.

One of the most important times of day for your brain is right before you drift off to sleep. Have you ever fallen asleep thinking about a song and then woken up with it still in your head? Or maybe you've gone to sleep pondering a problem and then woken up with a solution. That's not an accident. That's neurology. That's how your brain works.

God told the Israelites in Deuteronomy 6:6-7, "These commandments that I give you today are to be on your hearts. Impress them on your children. Talk about them when you...*lie down and when you get up.*" When you look at the neurology of sleep and the power of the human brain to solidify memories and think creatively during sleep, "when you lie down and when you get up" turns out to be the very best time to plant the things of God into a child's head. That's actually brilliant neurology. It's like God understood how the brain works. Interesting.

Whether you spend all day with your kids, or your family is separated from early drop-off to pick-up right before dinner, you have the opportunity to spend <18> of the most important minutes of their day with them—the <18> minutes right before they go to sleep.

Actually, you could start the day you find out that you are pregnant because babies can hear in the womb. They are born already knowing the songs you sing to them, the voices that talk lovingly to them, the voices that raise their mother's cortisol level. They will turn toward the faces that have spoken kindly to the mother and they will turn away from the faces that have spoken angrily to her.

<18> minutes is a nice memorable number for our purposes here, but it isn't a magical amount of time. You could spend half an hour or five minutes. <18> minutes is nice, though, because it's long enough to really let the kids feel comforted that you took time out of your electronically-directed day to look them in the eye and listen to them. It's also short enough to fit it into the inevitably busy evening schedule.

You may already be using this evening time to read a Bible story or pray with your kids. That's great! I think there are a few other simple additions that could make a life-changing difference. These will not just help your stress level (that's a nice bonus, maybe a life-saving bonus, depending on your family history), but they will also form life-long patterns of bringing ourselves to the arms of our loving God each night.

During these <18> minutes consider doing these five simple steps I call the "FAITH5" (Faith Acts In The Home):

1. Share a high and low from your day
2. Read scripture
3. Connect your highs and lows to the Scripture

4. Pray together
5. Bless each other

If you want more resources on each of them, visit www.faith5.org or read my book, *Holding Your Family Together*. The book is full of examples, stories, and science. The following is a good overview.

SHARE a High and Low

If we don't know someone's highs and lows, we don't really know that person. If we don't know our own highs and lows, we don't really know ourselves. It's important for humans to process the good and the bad in our lives. To name the things we are thankful for and to acknowledge the things that caused us pain. This obviously can give us insight into our kids. It can also be a chance for them to witness our highs and lows on a daily basis.

IF WE DON'T KNOW OUR OWN HIGHS AND LOWS, WE DON'T REALLY KNOW OURSELVES.

Some nights my wife and I could only reference our low in front of the kids because it was about something very personal between us. We used discretion, but we felt it was important to honestly model how it looks to live out the advice that I kept telling them, "People who love each other talk."

I wanted this base of communication between us and our teenagers so that when things became rocky as the hormones hit and the independence grew, they had already heard and seen that "People who love each other talk." If they see it every night, it might stick with them.

Highs and lows are also a wonderful way to work towards "Never let the sun go down on your anger." There were nights that I really wanted to hold a grudge against my wife, but as we sat there and Arlyce and I listened to each other share, the anger melted away. *Ah, that's why he was acting like that. Ah, that's what she needed.*

READ God's Word

My highs and lows alone are not enough to build an unshakeable foundation.

This is what I believe: If the Word of God is not true, then we have nothing. If it is true, then I'm going to trust it more than I trust myself, and more than I trust my circumstances.

You could take this time to tell the scripture stories to your kids, stories like Sarah, Paul, or baby Jesus. Or to read one verse together. Or—imagine this revolutionary idea—to *memorize* scripture together!

If your kids are young, you could take a verse and repeat it all week to let it soak in. You could use a verse that we have set to music, which will make it a breeze to memorize, even at *your* age!

You could choose a verse or a story from your personal Bible study. If you don't know where to begin, we have created a list at Faith Ink that covers all the big topics in the course of one year. This list is included in the appendix.

Saturate your children with the stories, the words, the symbols, and the things of God.

The only way we can recognize a counterfeit is to be saturated with the real thing. The way they train bank tellers to know the difference between real and counterfeit money is to saturate them with real currency.

How can we possibly hope that the next generation will follow the way of God if they don't know the way of God, the will of God, and the command of God?

TALK: Relate Highs and Lows to the Scripture

Simply speaking our highs and lows aloud before bed has many benefits. It is a great way to start our brains processing those things. Your brain can set to work on them overnight. Simply acknowledging a hurt in the safe presence of parents can prevent much tossing and turning in the dark alone.

But we can do more than just say our joys and sorrows out loud. Each night we can take our highs and lows to scripture. We can let our scripture reading and our high or low sit next to each other and see if there is any insight or comfort to be gained. This doesn't mean we have to go out of our way to think of the perfect verse or story to relate our child's high or low for the day. If something comes to mind, that's fine. Simply take a minute to let the scripture verse or story exist next to our high and low, and ponder them for a minute. We can take our highs and lows to the God who is there for us in both.

Bringing our highs and lows to scripture shows our kids that there is a place they can turn to when life gets rough or confusing. When they are older, in the wee hours of the morning tossing and turning because of a low, and we are not there to share the burden with them, they will have a place to turn. After 18 years of this, they'll be in the practice of taking their highs and lows to God's Word.

PRAY for one another's highs and lows

Taking our highs and lows directly to God in prayer at the end of each day is one of the most powerful things we can do before we close our eyes to sleep.

I try to go to sleep each night thinking: *I have done all I can do on this problem for today. I'm turning it over to you, God, and I'm going to bed.*

There are no stronger arms in which I can rest.

Bringing a sorrow or a request to God might be something you're familiar with, but bringing our joys to God is powerful as well. Our highs, our highlights of each day, don't erase the lows, certainly, but listing things for which we are thankful can give us much needed perspective.

Many nights Arlyce would simply sigh and say, "My high today is that Jesus loves me. Next." At the end of a difficult day, she was taking a moment to ponder that the God who created stars loves Arlyce. The God who created a world in which light and sound travel at different speeds loves Arlyce. The God who brings to bloom fields of wildflowers on mountaintops, just for his eyes alone, loves Arlyce. This is a good thing to put in the forefront of your brain as you're drifting off to sleep. The day's troubles may remain in your thoughts, but adding the idea that God loves you to the mix might help you say, *I'm turning this problem over to you, God. Goodnight.*

BLESS one another before turning out the lights on the day

Many faith traditions have incorporated the idea of blessings into their worship and even into their daily routines.

We can bless each other in many different ways, but today I'm going to talk about incorporating **a blessing word** and **a blessing touch**. **Blessing our kids** and having our **kids bless us.**

Some faith traditions incorporate practices you might think of as a traditional blessing: a minister laying his hand on a parishioner's head with a "May God bless you, my child." Other traditions might lay a hand on the shoulder of a person as they are being prayed for.

Maybe you grew up receiving the sign of the cross on your forehead. That might seem connected only to mainline traditions, but long before Jesus himself walked the earth, God was telling the Israelites to put the symbols of God on our foreheads:

> *Tie them as symbols on your hands and bind them on your foreheads.*—Deuteronomy 6:8

We could make a sign of the cross on our child's forehead after a prayer, just a mere quarter-inch away from their wrinkled neo-cortex, saying, "May God bless you tonight with good sleep." Or "May God keep you safe." Or simply, "You are loved by God." We could make the mark of the cross on their hands, where they'll be doing their work in the morning.

A safe, honoring touch, like a kiss on a toddler's forehead at the end of the night, speaks in a way that words alone cannot.

A SAFE, HONORING TOUCH, LIKE A KISS ON A TODDLER'S FOREHEAD AT THE END OF THE NIGHT, SPEAKS IN A WAY THAT WORDS ALONE CANNOT.

Every family has different ways they incorporate physical touch in their lives, but let us not forget to use this important language in our increasingly virtual world.

This blessing touch is not only something we can give, it is also something we can receive from our children. The toddlers that I know love to mark little crosses on the heads of their parents and grandparents. The weight of the world can seem so heavy at the end of the day, but it might help unburden some of that load if we look into the eyes of a child as they mark a cross on our forehead and say, "God bless you tonight, Mom." "God keep you tonight, Dad."

"OK, we tried all of this, but nothing that important happened."

Do not give up. The point isn't to make each night the most memorable night of your lives. The point is to create a routine that will be there to carry you when you cannot carry yourself. You are creating a habit of being honest with yourself, and in prayer with God, and with your inner circle, spouse, kids, or parents.

You will never know which day is that important day, when they have a low buried deep in their hearts. Maybe they won't know how to tell you over a busy dinner, but in this routine you can create a space where your kids are in the habit of sharing honest highs and lows. You will have the most well-adjusted kids on the block!

As an added bonus, they'll be in the habit of listening to the hearts of others.

You can practice these FAITH5 any time of the day.

There are many neurological and practical reasons to do this routine at bedtime. It can cut off stress or anger, and it can replace spiraling worries with God's promises and a family's love.

But the pieces can be transplanted to another time of day, or into other relationships.

Bob and his family do highs and lows at mealtime. He asks people to share a highlight and a prayer request, or to share a low if "prayer request" feels too weighted. He recently spent Easter in Alaska, where he was speaking at some high schools. He continued his tradition with his new acquaintances around the Easter dinner table.

I was recently at a dinner where people shared what they called a "world low." They mentioned something that was happening in the world that made them quite sad. That is a great way to encourage honesty and openness, but still keep up your personal boundaries. If a story is too personal, it can still be a relief to just have a forum in which to say, "I have a very difficult thing going on with my brother." It can be a way to break down the walls of isolation that pain can bring. Of course, it's always important to allow *anyone* to opt out.

We could also think about sharing highs and lows with our friends over coffee. It doesn't have to be as formal as going around in a circle and sharing a high and low, but think about asking and about sharing more than just sports news or dance class info.

Then after we talk about highs or lows, we can include any of the other pieces that seem to follow naturally. We could share God's Word and talk about how the high or low intersects with that word.

We could even ask to pray with them or for them. There are certainly a lot of circumstances where asking to pray for a stranger feels inappropriate, but I think we have unfortunately stopped thinking about it *at all.* We have stopped asking the Holy Spirit if this could be a time to ask to pray for them. We are too busy thinking about dinner and traffic and solving that problem at work. Who has time to think about eternity?

We can even bless people with our words and touch. I'm not suggesting putting your hand on a stranger's head, or making the sign of the cross on their forehead. But I think most people are not touched enough in this electronic world we live in. A hand on their shoulder, a handshake or even a hug, if appropriate, might mean a lot to someone. A kind word, certainly, would be a welcomed parting gift.

FAITH5 at bedtime will look different as your kids enter different ages and seasons, but it's worth creating the ritual and adjusting it over time.

Bob still practices these things to this day, even though most of Bob's kids don't live at home anymore. Whenever he has his family over for dinner, they still do highs and lows around the table. He said to me, "Life is just really busy for everyone. You'd be surprised at how little I'd really know about their highs and lows if we didn't take the time to do this."

Go diving for <18> minutes.

When you can, put your phone away, at least for your <18> right before bed. Leave the phone out of the room. We are living deeper and deeper in a fast-paced, technology-driven lifestyle. Or perhaps, I should say, we are living *shallower and shallower.*

Nicholas Carr in his book *The Shallows* compares the world we live in with a speedboat. We zip across the surface. We can go places and see things never before possible. It is thrilling. It is exhilarating. But it's not that deep. It is a surface-based life. You can't go deep on a motorboat. You just bounce along the top.

What if for <18> minutes each night, we turned off the motor and dove into the sea? To see.

What if we silenced the cell phone, left it in the other room, and went snorkeling with our kids? What if we took <18> minutes to see what life is like in the deep.

I know it's not realistic for most people to unplug for days or even hours at a time. To live beyond the constant access of the cell phone is practically an ancient way of life. I was reminded of this recently when I had one day in Boston in the middle of a busy travel itinerary. I had an upcoming book deadline to meet, so I stayed in my room. I turned off my Wi-Fi. I turned off my phone and poured myself into my work.

It happened to be the day of the Boston Marathon bombing. My wife heard the news instantly, just like most of the country did. She immediately began calling me.

By the time I turned my phone on, I had twenty-three messages from her. The first one was a bit frazzled, "Hey, honey, did you hear what happened? Call me back. I love you." By message twenty-three she was assuming the worst. We had a friend who was running that day, and she thought I had gone down to watch the race.

Now I always let her know if I'm going off-grid, because you never know what a day might bring. We live in a world where being off the grid for ten hours can be legitimate cause for concern, but even so, our technology doesn't have to own us.

For <18> minutes each night we can be free-range people. We can take these last moments of the day, which also happen to be some of the most powerful moments of the day, to do some of our most important work—being honest in sharing highs and lows with each other, reading God's word, talking about our highs and lows in reference to God's Word, praying together, blessing and being blessed by each other. That will make for a good night.

In a nutshell:

Spend time each night with your family practicing the FAITH5: sharing your highs and lows, reading scripture, relating your highs and lows to scripture, praying, and blessing.

2. SKYPE GRANDMA

#BobLenz

I was speaking at a conference a few years ago. I explained a little bit about the <18> campaign from the stage. I explained that we're trying to reach kids under the age of eighteen with the good news of Jesus.

After I spoke, a small woman with silver hair walked right up to me and said, "If you turn that <18> around, that's my age! I'm eighty-one, but you know, I feel eighteen on the inside!"

Even if you're not quite eighty-one, maybe that resonates with you. Maybe you still feel young at heart. Perhaps you have had a moment in your life when you saw some old guy across the room at your college reunion and then you realized, "Oh, I went to college *with* that guy. *We're the same age! I guess that is how old I am now!*"

Sometimes we think that people who are a lot older or a lot younger than we are belong to a totally different species. We think they are somehow not like us.

There are many cultures that hold their elders in high respect, but in America today, we tend to glorify youthfulness.

We want to look as young as possible, for as long as possible. We tend to celebrate child prodigies instead of experienced elders. It is more common to see a magazine headline that reads *30 influencers under 30* than it is to see a title like *6 game-changers in their 60s.*

When we do think about our older population, the thoughts that come to mind tend to be more about their needs than about what they have to offer. We focus on the medical needs, or the companionship needs, but we don't often think about our elders as one of our best resources. I hope we can turn that around because no society in the history of the world, who treats the elders the way we treat ours, has survived.

Rich puts it this way, "Every generation has gifts and needs."

RICH PUTS IT THIS WAY, "EVERY GENERATION HAS GIFTS AND NEEDS."

While parents are often busy with the numerous details in life (like working to keep food on the table), your grandparents may have the time to attend to the finer things in life, like ice cream in the afternoon, long conversations over extra-cheesy grilled cheese sandwiches, figuring out how to make large bubbles with a bubble wand, or making whatever—I mean, *whatever*— you want for your birthday meal.

In fact, when my mom became a grandma, she would invite our entire family over for lunch on Sundays, and she took the time to make about five different meals. She knew that Tim didn't like casserole, so she made pizza for him. She knew Amber loved roast beef. Some of the grandkids only liked hamburgers and hotdogs, and sometimes she even made up some fish for Dad. Basically, she made sure that everyone had their favorite food. Who would take the time to do these things? Who knew all those needs? Grandma did.

#RichMelheim

There is this story in the gospels about a trip Jesus took with family when he was twelve. The entire family traveled to Jerusalem, and when it was time to leave the city, Jesus did not go with them, but instead he stayed behind at the temple, preaching out of the scriptures. His parents were about two days into the journey home before they even *noticed* he was gone.

How could that be?

How could Mary have let this happen? We're talking about Mary, the woman God handpicked out of all of humanity to give birth to the son of God. How could Joseph have not noticed? This is Joseph, who, time and again, went above the call of duty.

It's easy to wonder how they could be so negligent. The thing is, it wasn't negligence. In the society in which they lived, their extended family was well, just like family. They were *all* looking out for each other, aunts and uncles looking out for nieces and nephews. Grandparents looking out for babies, and babies giving grandparents very real and important work to do.

In fact, that way of life is how families have lived for most of human history. It was not until the last seventy years or so that we've decided that one person, or one set of people, should be considered solely responsible for the life of another human being. We now expect these one or two adults to provide food and shelter and care for a child without any built-in support system. They are not expected to rely on aunties or uncles. A back-up system of grandparents is considered a luxury now. How is that even *possible*?

Hear me, please, I'm not suggesting that parents aren't currently doing an incredible job at it. They are. They are doing unimaginably well. What we are asking a mother, a father, or even a set of parents to do, has never been asked of them throughout time.

So, if it feels incredibly hard to you, *it is!* It is a monumental task. It is nearly impossible to have the brain space after months of sleepless nights to have edifying conversation with your children before they go to bed. It is a herculean task to ask you to provide food and shelter for your children *and* patiently let them practice using their little pincer grip while spaghetti gets all over their chair and your floor All the while keeping the bathroom reasonably germ-free.

Even with two committed parents, the task is more than has ever been asked of you.

If you sampled families living across the globe today, you'd find that this way of living so independently is not how every family lives. Even in the United States, many cultures still live with multiple generations interacting with dependence on each other, sometimes even living in the same house.

The more recent trend of young adults returning to live at home after college is perhaps a way we are dipping our toes back in that water. Needing each other is okay.

#BobLenz

I know there are many who have very difficult situations with their extended families. I know a young mother who lost her own mother to cancer before she had her first child. She grieves with each milestone that her mother isn't there to be Grandma, to share the joy and to give her advice. Thousands of miles separate other friends from their grandchildren. Or perhaps a disagreement or wound has cut a deep rift that is not easily healed. Perhaps you are hoping for reconciliation but must wait for your parents or your children to accept you back.

I did not have the easiest relationship with Carol's father. Some of the beliefs we had about God differed, and he was not very open to hearing our views.

A few years after Carol and I got married the tension had not subsided, but even so I continued to reach out to him. "You have a wonderful daughter, sir."

"Yeah," he said to me, coldly staring off in the distance. "We had high hopes for her until you came along."

We could have told ourselves that we had many reasons

to stop honoring him. We could have said, "He wasn't open to listening to us. He was not using wisdom in some of the decisions he was making."

It would have been easy to simply not be around him anymore, but I saw the need for my own kids to still be in a relationship with him. I wanted them to see the many positive things about him: his work ethic, his daily prayers, and his faithfulness and commitment to what he believed, even if it was different than what I believed.

Carol and I agreed that instead of arguing about the different expressions of Jesus, we would continue to express Jesus and represent Jesus in how we treated each other, young or old. We wanted to be really cross+generational, to center on what Jesus did on the cross and to lay down our lives, to pick up our own cross and to serve. So we continued to spend weekends with Carol's parents. We built up a good relationship with them to the point that, not too long before Carol's dad died, he said to me, "I think I found an exception for you in this faith thing." His voice was noticeably softer. "The Bible says, 'true religion that's acceptable is this: helping the widows and the orphans.' And you've done a lot of good, so I think your faith might be real."

We had different ways of expressing it, but we got down to what matters: faith in Jesus lived out in love. But so many times we focus on the pain of hurtful words, or not being respected, and we want to attack back instead of saying, "God has put these people in our lives, let's grow together in what it means to love God and to love one another."

It's not fair when you have to be the adult and love

your parents the way they ought to love you. I know so many who are in that situation. It's not fair. Yet, if you are able to have a safe relationship with them, there can be a lot of good there, even if there are many points of disagreement.

If you're lucky enough to live near your grandparents or your children's grandparents, be open to being dependent on each other for things. Of course, also be open to being *dependable*. Needs and gifts should flow both ways.

NEEDS AND GIFTS SHOULD FLOW BOTH WAYS.

If you're lucky enough to be a grandparent, you have an incredible gift to give to your grandchildren and your children. Your time and attention is an invaluable gift, even if you don't have a lot of time to give.

My children went to elementary school right across the street from my mom's house. The kids got a special pass to leave school during the lunch hour and eat at Grandma's house. They had hamburgers and vanilla milkshakes almost every day. That's not what *I* ate for lunch when I was a kid! That's a grandma for you.

Grandma Lenz would always sit with her grandchildren at the kitchen table as they talked over lunch. One day, when Joyel was nine, she was talking with Grandma Lenz about how she was really sad about some of her friends who were picking on her at school, and she didn't know what to do.

Grandma Lenz said, "Well, ya gotta love 'em."

"Yeah," Joyel said, "But I'm *mad* at them, I don't understand how I could love them."

Then my Mom went through the gospel with Joyel, explaining that Jesus died on the cross even though we didn't deserve it and even though we *still* do things that hurt people. He wants to forgive us for all of these things. He wants us to show that forgiveness to others, so that other people can know that God loves them too.

It was at that moment when Joyel thought, *OK. I want to do that. I want to make it my own. I want to tell my friends why I love them even when they're mean or bullying me.*

Grandma Lenz prayed with Joyel right there.

My mom was there for that incredible moment with Joyel. What a special thing she would have missed out on if my mom told us, "Oh, no, I don't want to feed your kids lunch every day. I've already put my time in." No one would have held that against her, but instead she chose to give her time during that lunch hour as a gift to her grandkids.

#RichMelheim

If you don't live near your grandparents, take full advantage of the technological world we live in and plan a call, Skype, Facetime or video chat with them once a week. I know a man who had to move across the country from his grandparents for his job, but he put it on his calendar every Sunday afternoon to call them and talk for a few minutes.

Every week his grandparents tell him about how appreciative they are that he called. His grandma still ends every conversation with a sincere, "Well, thank you for calling long distance!" He doesn't bother to explain that a *long distance* call isn't any more expensive than a local call on his cell phone plan.

The call is good for him too. It can be lonely to be in a work-obsessed culture thousands of miles from any family. Needs are being met on both ends of that long distance call every week.

If you are a grandparent, you could adopt grandkids, too. You could even adopt a youth group! My daughter's youth group had two older women who regularly went as chaperones on the youth retreats. One was loud and kept the teenagers up until two in the morning talking. She slept in a sleeping bag on an uncomfortable bunk, just like the teenagers. She was the one who wore crazy hats and went tobogganing, racing the kids down the hill. The other woman was quieter and was the one they turned to for deep conversations. Many different kinds of gifts are needed.

If it feels like a chore to you, try to reframe it. Think about what needs you have that an older or younger generation can gift to you. Think about what gifts you have that are needed.

You can also adopt a grandparent. I know a young mother who moved away from her family right after her first child was born. She noticed that the elderly man who lived across the street took care of his wife with dementia. She felt that she ought to spend more time visiting with him, and helping him around his yard. She visited him a few times, but she was pretty overwhelmed with being a new mother and all the daily changes that brought. She told me that as she looked at back at her journals from that time, she saw the old man and herself in a new light.

At the time, she felt that *she* was the one helping. She wanted to help him more, but couldn't find the space in her life to do it.

As she looked back in her journals, she saw that *he* was the one who was helping *her*. He had brought her lily bulbs in the spring. Bulbs that he dug up himself from his garden for her brand new yard. He was always overjoyed to receive her and her smiling baby as guests in his living room, and he brought out cookies for them to enjoy while they talked.

She realizes now how relieved she was to get out of the house and how special it was to go to a place where her loud child was welcomed. He would stop and talk to her in the grocery store line, unhurried and unworried, and ask her how she was and how he could pray for her. In this new town full of strangers, he was someone who remembered her name and details about her life.

She told me she wished she could go back and tell herself to *receive more help*: to visit him more. She wished she could have seen those cookie trays and conversations as a gift, a respite from a long day with an infant.

At the time she felt like it was intrusive to go visit him, but in hindsight she sees they were both taking care of a loved one by themselves, often stuck in the house on the dark, cold winter days. It would have been nice for both of them if she had taken him up on his offer more often. They would have both enjoyed more trays of store-bought cookies and conversation interrupted occasionally by the repeated questions of his wife slipping into dementia or by the cry of a baby. This, of course, would have been a gift to him, too, as the lone caregiver to his wife in a big house in the long winters.

If your grandparents are far away, love on them in whatever way you can. It's also OK to find surrogate grandparents, close at hand. Maybe their grandchildren are far away too.

When I was about twelve, a Chinese family moved into our town, they were the only Chinese family in Willioton, North Dakota. The father was a doctor and the mom didn't speak any English at the time. They had five kids and my parents pretty much adopted them as our relatives. My mom taught the mother English, and they taught her how to cook Chinese food. The kids beat me at ping-pong all the time. Dr. Cheng's brother was also a doctor and moved to town soon after.

Dad became their pastor. Dad baptized them, taught and confirmed each of the children. He helped them get acclimated to the small Upper Midwest town, and he helped the quiet, old Norwegian farmers and ranchers to be accepting of this new family. He just loved that family. My dad loved different cultures, and their friendship was a gift to him too in that homogeneous northern prairie.

Thirty years later, Dr. Cheng was retired and living in Los Angeles. Four of his five kids were doctors. Dr Cheng called up Dad and said, "I want to fly you out to California to bless all of my grandchildren one by one."

My dad got this call a short time after my mom passed

away. She had fallen and broken her hip. She did not survive the surgery. Dad was broken and displaced.

He took Dr. Cheng up on his offer and went to California all alone on a plane. He was met by this family, who years ago had joined our family around Thanksgiving and Christmas tables. Dr Cheng's adult children each told their old pastor how he had strengthened them in Christ and how honored they would be if he would bless their kids.

Dr. Cheng and his wife knelt down, and my dad put his hands on them and prayed for them and blessed them. Their kids, now adults, knelt couple by couple, and my dad put his hands on them, blessed them and prayed for them. Then one by one, each grandchild knelt down and my dad, who just became a widower, placed his hand on their heads and prayed a blessing over each of them, one by one.

Dad came home from that trip healed. The old pastor needed to be the channel of grace. He needed to be valued and needed to be validated.

Fifteen years after that trip, my dad was living in a dementia unit, in the final months of his life. It was the Fourth of July. My sister was having a picnic, so we brought him out of the care center to sit with us in the backyard under the shade of the big trees.

I had a broken arm. I was rushing out of town early one morning a few weeks earlier, trying to catch a flight to Seattle, and I crushed my arm in a freight elevator. Dad was just sitting there next to me, patting my arm. He didn't know my name, but he knew I was somebody special.

"Will you pray for my arm, Dad?"

"Dear Lord, you have the power of healing." The words came slowly and quietly, and I can still feel the gentle pat, pat, pat, up and down my cast. "Richard needs healing, in Jesus' name, I say, Amen."

He called me by name. Something he hadn't done in months.

"What's your advice for pastors?" I asked, wondering if more would come back to him.

Dad paused, like he was wading through fog. I waited for him to remember. After all, it was a national holiday. That's what we do on national holidays. We remember.

"Study," he said softly and gently.

"When I was ordained, you gave me two pieces of advice. 'Preach a good sermon and make sure they know you love them. And if they know you love them, then the sermon doesn't even have to be that good.'" I chuckled at the recollection. It was good advice.

"What has the most meaning for you?" I asked, seeking his thoughts on a project I was working on about the meaning of meaning.

Long pause. I waited again.

He looked right at me for the first time in this conversation. "You."

"Will you bless me?" I asked my dad and I gently placed his hand on my head, and we sat there, Dad breathing in that way the elderly do that makes you realize what a gift each breath is. After a moment, I stood, and leaned over to kiss him and hug him. Then I put my hand on his head and blessed him.

"God bless you, Dad."

As I took a deep breath and sat down, Dad looked right at me again and labored to say, "I love you, Richard."

He died three months later.

AS I TOOK A DEEP BREATH AND SAT DOWN, DAD LOOKED RIGHT AT ME AGAIN AND LABORED TO SAY, "I LOVE YOU, RICHARD."

HE DIED THREE MONTHS LATER.

In being asked to give a blessing to Dr. Cheng's family, my father received healing for one of the deepest wounds in his life, the loss of his wife. In being asked to give advice and blessing to me, my dad's brain pushed through the dementia for a few minutes, and he was present in that moment with us again. In my gifting some time and attention to my dad, (who had, according to all evidence available, forgotten me), I was given one of the happiest memories of my life.

In a nutshell:

Invest in meaningful cross+generational relationships.

3. COMMIT TO A SMALL CIRCLE OF FRIENDS

#RichMelheim

Before we dive into talking about why this experience is so important, I want to pause at the beginning and explain what we mean by the term *small circle of friends.* In our definition, it's four or five other family units who are intentionally and regularly part of your life.

Most churches have some kind of "small group" ministry these days, though it can bear many different names: community groups, life groups, home groups. It is not necessary that this group is formed through your church, though it's possible your church small group might become your lifelong circle of friends. We're not advocating any specific system or schedule. It is worth noting that this isn't a group that you meet with for just one year. Those more temporary circles can play many valuable roles in our lives, but we're going to focus on the many benefits to having a small circle that remains in your life through decades.

For one family that I know, their extended family is their small group. They live close enough together to be actively involved in each other's daily lives: attending games, faithfully having family birthday parties, and regular weekend gatherings. The kids in this family are growing up with many aunts and uncles in their inner, trusted circle, and the adults have lots of support from each other.

The small group, actually, is modeled after the extended family. In the days Jesus was walking on earth, the extended family was called the *Oikos*. It was primarily an economic unit. They were all bricklayers, or maybe tent-makers. They were looking out for each other, because at that time, it just was too much for one family to survive on their own.

What if we had an *Oikos* looking out for us? What if there were eight other voices saying, "Well, I wonder why your mother was so upset about that." Or, "When she was sixteen she was a little hellion too. I think there's hope for you." Grandma and Mom might have opposite opinions about what you should do, but they both have your best interest at heart. When you see caring adults disagree on something in a healthy way, you get to learn about making choices from two good options.

Having an *Oikos* today could take on many different forms. It could be a small circle of friends, or an extended family (either related family or adopted family). Bob and I each have a circle we have been meeting with regularly for more than twenty years. The way each of our groups have chosen to meet together, and how we've remained in each other's lives, has changed over the years, as our life stages changed.

Neither of our groups started out with a lifelong commitment. That would put a lot of weird pressure on those early meetings! Even now, we've never taken any oath or pact, but we have found our groove, and we've realized we needed to stick it out when things got rocky. Let me tell you, they *did* get rocky.

In a Christian culture that equates a high number of attendees with success, the importance of these long-term relationships can be easily overlooked. Small groups may be encouraged to disband as couples grow and mature in order to utilize them as new small group leaders.

There is obviously a tension of truth here. *Yes*, we are called to *go out*. We should not sit facing inward all the time and ignore the new families at church. Nor should we ignore the neighbor families down the street, nor the homeless guy who has mental health issues. The purpose of huddling up is to make our plan to go out and make the play. The huddle isn't the game; the huddle is so that we can play the game.

But there is *no* replacement for long-term relationships. In America where the average person will move more than eleven times in their lifetime[6], and have four job changes on average before age thirty-two[7], we have an increasingly great void for long-term relationships.

Aside from all the life changes that make long-term relationships more difficult in our culture, relationships themselves can be complicated. Conflict will definitely arise. It can be easier to say, "We're growing apart. I'm going to find a *new and better* friendship with someone who is *more like me*."

It *is* good and wonderful to find new friends. Bob and I are relatively recent friends. There is a distinct thrill of a new friendship. Everything is interesting, everything is wonderful, everything is exciting. Yet, as men who have stood by our friendships for decades, we plead you to consider the gifts that can only come out of those long-term relationships.

Think about what you might be facing five years from now, or ten years, or twenty years.

Think about the support you might want in place when your child hits the teenage years, when you and she may not be able to find a way to talk about something. What if she could have in her life four or five other women who have known her since she was a small girl? They could be ears to listen to her heart and mouths to speak words of kindness that you might have a hard time speaking. They could echo your words of wisdom that she might have difficulty hearing from you. And they could affirm to her that you love her deeply.

Think about when your marriage faces changes and trials. What invaluable grace it is to have friends who know you and your spouse, who can speak both assurance and hard truth as needed.

Think about when you will face great loss. Those are the times you will want someone who *already* knows you. You need someone close enough to you to come help with practical everyday needs, when you are so steeped in grief that you can't even reach out for help. You need someone who knows your heart so well they can sit with you quietly in your loss. It is a small comfort in these times to be known and seen and remembered in the depth of grief, but it is one of the few comforts available.

#BobLenz

Carol and I were invited by a friend to join three other couples for a weekend at a cabin up North. We were sitting around the fire and realized that everyone was a leader of some type of ministry. Some of us were full-time ministers and others were volunteer worship leaders or Bible Study leaders. We talked about how we needed a place we could go and not be in charge of anything. We needed a place where we didn't have to minister to everyone and we could truly let our guards down. So we started to meet together every other week. We all took turns hosting, so you only had to lead when you were hosting. I think the sharing of this leadership and responsibility is part of the reason why we've been able to continue meeting together for so long.

This group has been great for many reasons, but during our times of grief we have really appreciated having them around. Carol and I have each lost both of our parents, and we were supported by our friends during this time. This support doesn't take the grief away, but life and death are both part of the journey. We have walked on the mountain-tops and in the valleys with our people, through highs and lows, as they have been there for us and we have been there for them.

Neither my group nor Rich's group set out in those earliest years to stay together for three decades, but through babies and teenagers, graduations and birthdays, illnesses and deaths, we have been immeasurably glad we did.

I know there are people in our community who look at us and think, "If I just was in a group like the Mavericks (yes, we named ourselves eventually), then my life would be better." I think that means we haven't been as honest as we could be about what it looks like to be in a small group like this.

My daughter, Joyel, might have a more realistic view of it, having seen and heard about much of it from the inside. She doesn't know everything, of course, but she has seen that we have deep differences in parenting styles and differences in how we value spending our money. She has seen that we've had to work out more than a few hurts over the years. She told me that now, in her small group with her husband, when something difficult comes up she is able to say, "Come on, guys, this is not something we're going to break up over." She has seen first-hand that creating lasting friendship requires a commitment to stay together. Even though it takes a lot of work, I want everyone I know to be able to experience a small group like the one I've had.

Jesus' ministry happened on the small scale and the large scale. On the smallest scale, he modeled taking time alone to be with God (fortunately for the introverts among us). Outward from there, three men were his closest companions, and beyond that he had a group of twelve disciples he traveled with. These twelve were specifically called and commissioned by him. They traveled closely with him and participated in much of his day-to-day life during his ministry on earth. Moving out from the twelve, there was a larger group of men and women who followed Jesus. We don't know many of their names, or exactly how many there were, since most of them were not recorded in scriptures or history books, but Jesus knew them. Beyond that large group of believers, of course, he ministered to crowds of strangers, some of whom he only saw once. Like Jesus, we can engage in sharing God's love with those we are very intimate with and with those we have just met.

The small circle we're talking about is about the size of group of the twelve disciples. And like them, this circle in your life should be people who are chosen purposefully — don't just pick a dozen random people at your church. It's right and good to use discernment here. They should be close to you in proximity. Though it is wonderful to have deep friendships far away, having people who know you deeply, and whom you bump into regularly in real life, is important. This group should be on the same mission that you are. This is where it can get a bit fuzzy. You're not going to find a dozen people who are exactly like you. It's actually *good* if they are quite different from you. It is important, though, for you to have most of your biggest values in life to be in common.

Having lived through many decades, I can tell you many of our families' most pressing issues have changed over time.

In fact, Rich told me a great story about how we change. He said he was meeting with a friend and in the course of their conversation, the science of the human body came up. (If you've ever had a conversation with Rich that will not surprise you. Every single conversation en*rich*es you).

Rich was telling this man that the male body replaces all of its cells over the course of about seven years (everything except the teeth). The female replaces everything over the course of five years. Each of our systems replaces at different rates. The top layer of skin is pretty fast, of course. But even our bones replace each cell so that not one single cell is left the same after seven years. Except your teeth–floss and brush!

The next day, this man went to be interviewed for the senior pastor position at a large church. The interview went exceedingly well, and at the end of it, with smiles all around the table, the committee asked him if he had any other questions or comments.

He said, "Well, just one final thing. I wanted to let you know that I've been married for 35 years, but this isn't my first wife." The smiles around the table of this very conservative church began to drop. "She is actually my seventh wife and I'm her fifth husband." You could hear some uncomfortable throat clearing in the room before he explained to them the science Rich shared with him.

He explained further, "Just like my wife and I, this church will change and grow over time. This church will not be the same body in five or ten years as she is today, but my commitment to her will remain. I will be committed, not just to the person she is now, but to the person she will grow to be."

We change every year, like our cells do. Some systems change quickly, some things change slowly over time. We should not enter any relationship with the false expectation that things will always stay exactly the same. We should not be surprised or abandon ship when things get a bit rocky.

WE CHANGE EVERY YEAR, LIKE OUR CELLS DO. SOME SYSTEMS CHANGE QUICKLY, SOME THINGS CHANGE SLOWLY OVER TIME. WE SHOULD NOT ENTER ANY RELATIONSHIP WITH THE FALSE EXPECTATION THAT THINGS WILL ALWAYS STAY EXACTLY THE SAME. WE SHOULD NOT BE SURPRISED OR ABANDON SHIP WHEN THINGS GET A BIT ROCKY.

The relationships that exist in our small circle of committed friends are good for our kids too. It was so great for my brave and extroverted daughter when she was young to have examples in our small group of strong, opinionated women who were leaders in their communities for good.

Sometimes people will compliment me about how incredible my wife is. I couldn't agree more. Carol is awesome.

She is a great listener and a real role model for how you can be an introvert and use those gifts to live a life of service to God. I'm so glad people recognize that even though she is different from me, her gifts are important in this world. I think those with quieter gifts can be often be undervalued in the church.

I hope people appreciate the extroverted gifts of my beautiful youngest daughter. She is incredible. She's confident, speaks boldly, and takes control of situations. She serves God with her life in different ways than my wife. Extroverted gifts can also be underappreciated, especially in women in the church.

I loved that my daughter had women she knew as she was growing up who had personalities like hers. My daughter and my wife had a *great* relationship, but we want to show our kids that to be a follower of Jesus, they don't have to look exactly like Mom or Dad. Our world and our families need each one of us to be the unique expression of God's love that God created us to be.

#RichMelheim

Arlyce and I have been part of a small group of couples that have been friends for nearly 30 years. Originally we began as a small group through our church. We've attended countless birthday parties, and more recently, many graduations and weddings for our children. I'm closer to many of their children than I am to my own nieces and nephews, who live many hours away. My work causes me to travel a lot, and the way these families have supported Arlyce while I've been away has meant a lot to me.

Though I'm an author and speaker now, when we were first married I was a youth pastor. Arlyce knew that this job often meant multiple moves over the course of a career. When our children were very young, we moved to Stillwater, Minnesota, and she was the instigating factor in our decision to stay in Stillwater until our children finished high school, to provide them some stability during their childhood. It was a difficult decision and meant we lost out on some opportunities. It also meant we began new things we otherwise never would have tried. One of the best things to come out of that stability is that we've built lifelong relationships with this circle of people.

YOU DON'T HAVE TO SIT DOWN WITH A GROUP OF TEN STRANGERS AND MAKE A BLOOD PACT TO STILL BE FRIENDS IN TWENTY YEARS. DON'T START THERE. BUT START *SOMEWHERE*.

You don't have to sit down with a group of ten strangers and make a blood pact to still be friends in twenty years. Don't start there. But start *somewhere.* Keep in mind that the idea of having a lifelong circle of friends is something that will nourish your life and the lives of your children. Imagine these friends with their arms around you as you weep for joy at your child's wedding or weep in sorrow at a loss. These relationships will play a big role in your child's future faith. They will hold you when you cannot hold yourself. They can hold your children when they are looking for arms to run to that are not your own.

#BobLenz

About one week before we sent this book to be published, a great tragedy hit one of the families in my small group. We woke to the news that one of our own, Al Rockman, had a heart attack during the night and went to be home with Jesus.

Though we know we will see him again someday, our grief is immense at this great loss.

Carla Nelessen, who is also in our small group, wrote down some of her thoughts as she processed her grief. She gave me permission to share them with you. I think she articulates well what it looks like to be in a small group as she honors the impact Al's extraordinary, everyday faith had on the people around him.

#CarlaNelessen

I was talking with my sister Mary Ann last night, and she said that sometimes it's best to let the grief overwhelm you. Sometimes it is best to just sit with it. That was so helpful. So often, I try to run away from the grief, and not allow healing.

I thought about Al and his contemplative nature. I'm so glad we were gifted with him as a friend. I realized this morning how much I take people for granted.

So many of my thoughts this morning were about who Al was to me as a friend. I suddenly became so aware of how his faith had impacted mine. All sorts of memories kept coming back: joyful, painful, contemplative, the jokes.

A few years ago, my husband and I took a vacation to Mexico together with Al and Mary Rockman. We celebrated on that trip through reading, rest, laughter, beauty, food, sunshine, games, boogie boarding in the ocean, volleyball (solidly beating a bunch of Canadian young folks), and great conversations.

Al was such a complex mix of practical, solid thinking and soul-filled worship. Recognizing God's design in creation, in music and in people was his specialty. And he was always heavenly minded. He had a peace about him even in the midst of gut-wrenching pain.

Al's biorhythms in life were to be an early-riser and nap-taker. So at sunrise, he often took walks along the ocean with God, and then picked out the lounge chairs for the rest of us late risers. He was always looking to serve. Sometimes he would try to explain to us about those times alone with the Lord, but it often became a far-off look in his eyes. He had a solid assurance that there is a better land, a better place.

I was envious of his faith. My faith was real and

sure, but it often took the posture of a complainer, or was angry, doubt-filled, and disappointed in unanswered prayers.

It was these conversations with Al, my ordinary friend, which spurred me to look deeper at, and long deeper for, this unseen God, who loves us more than we can imagine, even in the midst of dark shadows of death.

We have been learning for a long time what living in community looks like. We, as a small group, needed an extended amount of time to learn this, I think, since it's been 26 years. In those 26 years, I have sabotaged, wounded, and have brought about the oxymoron of "divided unity" as much as any normal sinner. Somehow, each member has forgiven me and given me grace, so that I could experience one of my all-time favorite verses in scripture, "Above all, love each other deeply, because love covers over a multitude of sins." 1 Peter 4:8. Having experienced it, I can now apply it to all messy relationships.

I must say, our small group has had very wonderful experiences together. We've celebrated graduations, weddings, cookouts, bonfires, pontoon rides, volleyball, music festivals, sponsoring children, mission trips, the ever popular Funyon Run, loads of games like Up & Down River or cribbage, and grandchildren (Let's just linger on new life and grandchildren for a moment).

We've also felt death, loss, change, heartbreak, anger, disrespect, disappointment, relationship crap, job changes, conflicts, and normal sinner things.

Twenty-seven years ago, Mark and I had relationships with each of these wonderful couples. However, I wanted more. So I prayed, and I asked for that. Oh, I received that and so much more.

Today, I read something from Henri Nouwen[8] that put it all into perspective. This describes what I am longing for and how Al lived it out.

> "Community is not easy. Somebody once said, 'Community is the place where the person you least want to live with always lives.' In Jesus' community of twelve apostles, the last name was that of someone who was going to betray him. That person is always in your community somewhere; in the eyes of others, you might be that person.
>
> Why is it so important that solitude come before community? If we do not know we are the beloved sons and daughters of God, we're going to expect someone in the community to make us feel that way. They cannot. We'll expect someone to give us that perfect, unconditional love. But community is not loneliness grabbing unto loneliness: 'I'm so lonely, and you're so lonely.' It's solitude grabbing onto solitude: 'I am the beloved; you are the beloved; together we can build a home.' Sometimes you are close, and that's wonderful. Sometimes you don't feel much love, and that's hard. But we can be faithful."

Al was always a great example of choosing to be faithful.

C.S. Lewis said, "Friendship is unnecessary, like philosophy, like art. It has no survival value; rather it is one of those things that give value to survival."[9]

Thank you, Al, for being a faithful husband, father, son, brother and friend. Thanks for your friendship. I will treasure it always. Now I carry with me a longing and hope for a better home and a deeper trust in God. That's what comes from an ordinary guy following an extraordinary God so closely.

And thanks for giving so much value to survival. I hope I can do the same for others. I will attempt to live it out. I know that's what you would want me to do.

In a nutshell:

Commit to a small group of friends who also commit to you and your kids.

4. A DOG'S BLADDER INFECTION, A KIDNEY TRANSPLANT, AND A WAITRESS

#RichMelheim

I was guest preaching at a church a few years ago. When it came to the time in the service for the prayer, I stepped down into the aisle among the congregants. I asked, "Are there any additional prayer requests this week?"

A young girl was the first to raise her hand, "Please pray for Sophia. She's my dog. She has a bladder infection."

We all smiled and I offered up a prayer right there for Sophia and her bladder.

After a moment, an older man raised his hand and asked for prayer for the continued function of his kidney. He was on the transplant list, and he had just been informed that he had a match. But when he asked about who was next on the list, he was told it was a young man with children. The elderly man passed on the kidney so it would go to this young father, though had never met him and never would meet him.

Kidneys don't become available very often, and his health was declining fast. That might have been his last opportunity.

He might have just sealed his fate. Those thoughts remained unspoken, but we understood that he needed prayer for both his kidney's health, and also for strength and comfort in the difficult and wonderful decision he had made.

We took a moment as a congregation and prayed.

After another moment, a woman raised her hand and asked for prayer for her friend who had been clean for six months and was trying to move out of her car and into an apartment. The woman said that her friend was on the path to putting her life back together. But paying for a deposit on an apartment, the first month's rent, and getting an apartment manager to approve you on waitress' paystubs weren't the easiest of accomplishments.

She said that her friend wanted to get into an apartment so that she could get her kids back.

The woman finished the prayer request about "her friend." I noticed the woman sitting next to her had tears streaming down her face.

We prayed for the woman's friend.

The woman who had been crying left the building right before the service ended.

I spoke afterward with my friend, Jack, who attended the church. He told me that she arrived late to every service and left early, though she had been faithfully attending every week for six months.

No one had gotten a chance to talk with her and find out her story because she was never there long enough, or early enough, to have a conversation.

Jack and I went out for lunch after church to watch

the Saints vs. Giants playoff game. We went to a local sports bar and, by chance (by God), our waitress happened to be the woman who was crying in church.

She recognized us and we recognized her. She told us she was, in fact, the "friend" that the woman had asked prayed for, as we had guessed.

Jack knew someone at church that owned some apartment buildings. He arranged a meeting, which led to her getting an apartment a few weeks later.

I want to be a part of a church like that.

I want for you and for your kids to be a part of a church like that.

A church that cares for a little girl's dog's bladder infection. A church that grieves and rejoices and prays with an elderly man in some of the final and most noble decisions he will make about his life. A church that joins in rejoicing and joins in grieving. A church that knows the highs and lows of its people.

I want for your church to see the needs of those who struggle in such a deep way that getting to church late and leaving early might be the very best they are able to do.

I want for your church to connect its people together to meet needs within the body. I want apartments to be filled with tenants and homes to be found for mothers and children.

This can play out in so many different ways. There is not a right size, a right worship format, a right sermon style. Taking prayer requests aloud on a Sunday morning is one way, but not the only way. How could your church do it? Be your unique reflection of God in your unique community.

In your own way, find out about your people and care for them in every single way you can.

The Saints beat the Giants, by the way, on that playoff Sunday.

In a nutshell:

> Be committed to a community of believers who are a unique and active expression of God's love for the people in their church and outside of their church.

5. SURROUND THEM BY A GREAT CLOUD OF WITNESSES

#RichMelheim

We don't spend a lot of time in our culture thinking or talking about death. It might seem cruel to our current cultural sensibilities to bring a child to a funeral. Yet, I've seen many kids sitting through PG-13 movies that could give them nightmares. I don't think that adds up.

And what about after the moment of death? And after the funeral? Christians believe in life after death, but the details of what this looks like are unclear. In a day where science reigns king, I think many find it difficult to figure out how to talk about something we cannot scientifically prove.

There is much disagreement amongst Christians about how this world will end. When I was young arguments about exact dates and times of how the world would end seemed to be a popular topic among some Christians. My mom was tired of the multitude of heated disagreements and would say to me, "Do you want to know the secret to understand the book of Revelations? Get a pencil, write this down. *God wins*. That's all you need to know!"

Yet, should we ignore everything after death? Does that mean we never think about what lies ahead or those who went before us?

"DO YOU WANT TO KNOW THE SECRET TO UNDERSTAND THE BOOK OF REVELATIONS? GET A PENCIL, WRITE THIS DOWN. *GOD WINS*. THAT'S ALL YOU NEED TO KNOW!"

In Hebrews, chapter eleven, Paul talks about the faith of *the ancients,* men and women of faith who had lived before. He begins chapter twelve this way: "Therefore, since we are surrounded by such a great cloud of witnesses, let us throw off everything that hinders and the sin that so easily entangles. And let us run with perseverance the race marked out for us."

The picture he paints is like a cheering crowd in a stadium. We are in a race, and we are surrounded in the stands by this great cloud of witnesses to God's faithfulness. We are surrounded, hopefully, by witnesses we can see in the flesh. Many of the other <18> experiences talk about ways to surround your child with a safety net of human witnesses to God's grace.

But the great cloud of witnesses goes beyond those with whom we can chat over coffee.

The ancients are also cheering us on. The stories of Abraham or Rahab in the Old Testament can cheer us on. Even Paul, who wrote that verse in Hebrews, is now also one of the ancients. Surround your child with their stories. Add these witnesses to the crowd cheering on your children.

Surround them with stories of *the ancients* of a more recent time—C.S. Lewis or Martin Luther King Jr. Take time to study their biographies and writings. There are so many unique faith stories. Find those personalities that intersect with your family's passions and interests.

Surround your children with the stories of their own *ancients*. Who were they named after? Did their great grand parents have faith? What struggles did they face? How did they overcome those difficulties? What was their greatest joy in life?

We can ignore death for a while, but not forever. We, of all people, have reason to look beyond death with great hope. Our God has gone before us into death and broken its power over us, turning death into a door to eternal life. Because of Jesus we have that life now. It begins here and continues on, beyond death. We don't offer faith to our kids as fire insurance. Yet it is the only thing that they can take with them through the grave and beyond.

And there we will be united with all the children of God. All those who have gone before and whose lives have encouraged us to keep running the race when it gets difficult. Don't forget to surround your child with these witnesses, their stories, and their lives. We pick up the baton from them, and when we see how far and fast and long they ran, it gives us the boost we need. We take a deep breath and keep running ourselves. We can "run with perseverance."

In a nutshell:

Share the stories of those who have gone before us.

6. WE DO LOUD REALLY WELL

#RichMelheim

When Bob, Nica and I were writing this book, we invested a day with my brilliant marketing friend, Bill Oeschler. After our late flights, we arrived at his doorstep at midnight and he greeted his hungry guests with a delicious pot of white chicken chili. We all turned from guests into friends as we listened to each other's hopes and dreams, and shared our disappointments and frustrations. (We shared our highs and lows, you could say.)

He told us the next morning, "I love doing hospitality because someone is a guest as soon as they enter the threshold of your house, but they become a friend as soon as you start sharing your lives together."

His love for hospitality was confirmed in the sight of two witnesses: the homemade midnight chili and a breakfast buffet which wrapped around half of the kitchen.

He became our friend very quickly while sharing his story. He could have solicited lots of *oohs* and *ahs* if he'd stayed in the safe realm of his impressive resume. His work and life experience is really quite something, but he did not choose to filter his life to look good. He was honest with us, and he also spent a lot of time listening. He asked us about what was on our hearts.

In the bathroom of Bill's house we noticed a wall hanging that says this:

"We do second chances.

We do mistakes.

We do forgiveness.

We do loud really well.

We do family.

We do love."

This reflects his home so well. We witnessed these things from the very personal vantage point of a houseguest. We passed fruit salad down the table between family members. We stacked plates in the dishwasher together, and we shared a bathroom.

Ah, sharing a bathroom. Now that's the real trick in any relationship, isn't it?

That's how we share our faith in Jesus with the next generation. Well, not by sharing bathrooms, exactly, but by having a place we all can get clean every day. And a place to get rid of the bad stuff.

We share our faith by having grace for each other in the process.

By doing forgiveness. Doing love. Doing loud really well. That's what FAITH5 is: being honest about who we are and taking our joys and sorrows to the God who loves us and is powerful enough to save us.

This made me think about a piece of art hanging above the dining room table at my friend Shannon's house. It says in beautiful chalk script:

**"We were delighted to share with you
not only the gospel of God
but our lives as well."**

These words come from a letter in the Bible which was originally penned by three friends and sent to a church in Thessalonica. We are to share not just the good news, but our lives, just like Jesus did with his disciples.

Our homes are places where we share the good news and our lives with *each other* and with *others*, inviting them into our spaces and going out together to other places.

Bob's family has a plaque in his house that says, "**Live, Laugh, Love**." That was a kind of family motto, or family mission for them for many years. They recently made a more detailed family mission statement:

The Lenz Home!

A place we long for Christ to be Lord.
A place to just be.
A place of refuge and rest in Him, so that all of life
becomes worship.
A place that values relationships.
A place where people matter.
A place of true J.O.Y.
A place you can have fun and party!
A place to share, be heard and understood.
A place to weep and share your needs.

A place to relax or be busy.
A place to work hard, play hard or do nothing.
A place to explore, question, learn, discover, challenge,
grow, even debate.
A place to be yourself.
A place to fail or succeed.
We seek to be welcoming and accepting.
We seek to be loving and respectful.
We seek to be authentic, real and intentional.
We seek to work through things, always with Grace
and forgiveness.
We value togetherness, yet with boundaries for being alone.
We value Faith.
We value each individual.
We value family, friends and community.
We value God.
We value Life.

What does your family do really well? Loud? Food? Does your family pool their money at Christmas to buy gifts from the wish list of a family at a local shelter? Or does your family provide a safe space for neighborhood kids to play? What does your family do well?

Where could you hang your family declaration? By the table where you share your meals with friends and strangers? In the main floor bathroom where you wash your hands daily? By the front door where you go out together and serve?

In a nutshell:

Be intentional about what your family values. Love each other and serve others in the unique way that only your family can. And for fun, create a family motto!

If you want to create a family motto, here are some suggestions:

1. **Plan a fun family meeting.**
    - Leave your cell phones in the other room.
    - Don't forget snacks!
    - Maybe art supplies would be inspiring.
    - Allow enough time for some goofy conversations to happen, even if they're not on-topic.
2. **Don't worry about picking the very best motto.**
    - You could choose a family motto for just one year.

- If you move to a new neighborhood or change schools, you could consider rethinking your family motto.
- You might find your "temporary" family motto sticks.
- Or maybe next year holds a new challenge you want to address.
- These are all good options!

3. **Answer any of these questions to get your ideas flowing:**
    - What do we love to do?
    - What has God put on our hearts?
    - How do we want to be described by people who know us?
    - What do we do really well?
    - What do we want to do really well?
    - What challenges do we face this year?
    - Is there a poem or song that sums up our hopes?
    - Is there a Bible verse that you love?
4. **Don't forget: there is no right or wrong answer!**
    - Short is OK
    - Long is OK too!

5. **Make a family motto sign (created by kids or adults) and hang in a spot of your choosing.**
    - On your doorframe?
    - In your living room?
    - By your table?
    - On a keychain?

7. PRACTICE RADICAL AND REAL HOSPITALITY

#BobLenz

The year Carol and I got married, we made a grand total of $3,000 between us. And we had a baby. And the hospital bill for that baby was about $3,000. We survived because people took care of us. Anonymous financial gifts and bags of groceries would show up at our house.

Things got better after that first year, but I had not chosen the most lucrative profession. We had to learn over the years how to use our money *very* wisely. We've done this mostly as a united front, but like any couple, we still have a few standard conflicts over cash flow. I complain that we spend too much money on the groceries. She answers back with a look of incredulity, reminding me that I'm the one who is always inviting people to our house. Relatives, hordes of teenagers, or even just late night board game opponents all get hungry and thirsty eventually.

When I was growing up, my mom's motto was: What's mine is yours. Everyone was welcome in our house. What we had, we freely gave. We do hospitality the way my mom did it. My daughter told me that her friends still talk about the love and safety they felt at our house. She says it really stuck with her that whatever things we had in our house, our kids and our guests could use.

But what do you do when you have a heart for radical hospitality and your reality is living on a frugal budget?

There was a season at Life Promotions, the non-profit I founded, where finances were very, very tight. I sat down with the board for an all day, difficult conversation about how we could make our expenditures match our income. At some point, we looked at staff benefits, like health insurance. I opened up discussion with a big sigh and this question: "Okay, what do we *have* to do? What are we obligated to do?"

Stan Plzak, one of the members of the board, calmly responded, "Well, Bob, I think the better question would be, 'What is the *best* we can do?'"

His wisdom stuck with me. I think that's a great way to think about hospitality, especially when you can't do *everything*. What is the best you can do?

WHAT IS THE BEST YOU CAN DO?

Bring what you have, even if it feels like it's as small as five loaves and two fish. Sometimes God multiplies our small gifts miraculously. Sometimes we discover that our small offering is sufficient for a need. It isn't about what you have, but who you trust and what you do with it.

Rich and I had a big discussion about how important

hospitality is when we stayed at Bill's house in Colorado. Bill served us fruit salad with sweet blueberries that were almost as big as gumballs. His breakfast was a five-star event and he stayed up well past midnight to greet us with hot soup after our flight was delayed, then delayed again. Bill practiced *radical* hospitality.

We, in turn, made a point to practice radical hospitality to others after we left Bill's house. Though, to be honest, this is something that runs in Rich's blood every week of the year. He regularly takes groups of creative people to mountain work retreats, where beauty and rest surround them. He makes meals for them. He makes fires in the fireplace just so you can hear the inspirational crackle of the wood as you wake up in the morning.

If you want to practice radical hospitality, you're not going to do it by accident. You have to be proactive.

#RichMelheim

For some reason, when I went on my pastoral internship, no one explained to me that I wouldn't get to go home for Easter and Christmas. That came as a big shock to me. But on the first Christmas that I ever spent away from home, the senior pastor felt sorry for my wife and me, a young couple alone in town. They had us over to the house for Christmas dinner. I'm sure my mother, who had invited over the lonely college students all those years, now appreciated someone taking in her son when he was far away.

This family even had presents under the tree for us.

Their little boy David opened one of his presents and when he saw the contents, he exclaimed, "Oh! Just what I *aaaalways* wanted ... but not very much."

"OH! JUST WHAT I *AAAALWAYS* WANTED ... BUT NOT VERY MUCH."

I thought that was a great way to think about hospitality. In our serving, are we giving what is *really* wanted? Or are we offering what they "always wanted...but not very much"?

When it comes to radical hospitality, you have to think of the *other*. What would *they* really like? What would make them feel at home?

The idea of radical hospitality means acceptance. It means that I'm not judging you. I want to have you around. It does not mean putting on a show. It doesn't mean you have to love every single thing about a person. Focus on something you can genuinely love.

Could you imagine how it would affect our communities and relationships if our homes were places of radical hospitality? If we decided this year, we're going to bring over the people we don't normally run into.

We're not going to be any less than who we are. We're going to be honest and real about who we are, what we believe, and why we do what we do. We're not inviting people over for dinner to sell them something, but if you think about giving your best as part of your radical hospitality, what is your best? What is the best thing you have to offer?

In Jesus' time on earth, the tradition was that the hosts would serve the best wine first to their guests, until it ran out. What is our best wine? For me, the best thing I have to offer is Jesus. I'm not going to hide it behind closed doors until you leave. I'm not just going to serve you grade-A steaks on the grill and topical, funny conversation. Those are like leftovers to me. These leftovers may be the best this world has to offer, but in the midst of it all, I'm not going to leave my "best wine" hidden in the pantry.

#BobLenz

Can you create an environment of radical hospitality if you're not on a mountainside in Aspen overlooking the sunset? What does it look like on a limited grocery budget?

For my wife Carol, it looks like hiding soda and snacks in our room under the bed.

She finds the deals on soda, and then she stocks up. Still to this day, she'll text my kids who live in town so they'll be aware of the great soda deals, so they can stock up too.

Of course, the problem with stocking up on soda is that if you open the fridge or the pantry and you see giant stacks of soda, what do you do? You happily take one and drink it. And that's exactly what the next person does, and the next person. At one point, there were eight of us living in that house. Carol and I, my five kids, and my sister Lois. It doesn't take eight people long to finish off a grocery cart full of soda. Then when my kids' friends would come over, there might not be anything left.

So Carol would reserve sodas and snacks and hide them under her bed, not for herself, but for her kids' loud, teenage friends!

That's pretty rad.

Sometimes people stop short of opening their homes and lives because we have this idea of what *Radical Hospitality* is, and it doesn't match up with the circumstances of our *Real Lives*.

My daughter told me that her friends loved to be at our house when they were teenagers because it was real. It wasn't new. It wasn't big, but it was real, and it could be lived in. We didn't have a lot, but what we had could be used. Couches could be sat on. Pizzas in the freezer could be eaten. Darts in the basement could be played. You could be yourself at our house. We would still rush around cleaning bathrooms before guests arrived, but the fact that the living room wasn't tidy wasn't going to stop us from opening our home.

Sometimes we need to rise to the challenge of practicing radical hospitality, and sometimes we need to be challenged to be more real. An important part of Bill's example of radical hospitality is his wife's example of real hospitality. She had a number of things she was committed to do with her kids early the next morning after our midnight flight. So when we arrived at the door, she was already in bed. She had stayed up quite late hoping to see us, but after our flight was delayed the second time, she knew she couldn't wait up. She knew we'd be in good hands with Bill and his chili. She welcomed us warmly that next morning over breakfast. She didn't offer some grand show. Her reality was that she needed a decent night's sleep for the many ways she would show her own radical and real hospitality in her real life the next day. She did not let her *real life* stop her from offering what she had. She and Bill worked as a team and were happy to welcome us into their very real home, during their very real life.

It can be easy to think, "When I am in the position to offer something truly amazing, I'll do it." If we are honest, the motivation for that might be more about making sure everyone will be so impressed by *us*, instead of letting our real, radical hospitality point to our God who sustains us.

We have many opportunities in our lives to love people the way God asks us to love. We can do it at our work, or through coaching at the YMCA, or teaching a pottery class. We can do it with our money or we can volunteer at church. But none of these will leave as deep an impression on our kids as the way in which we welcome people into our homes, and how we treat them when they are there.

That's our home base. It's our most vulnerable spot and it's where we keep everything that is most important to us. Are we real in our homes? Do we invite young couples over to witness an older marriage interact over the making of dinner, and the setting and clearing of the table? Do we invite our real friends to wash dishes with us in our untidy kitchens? Are we radical in our love? Do we love others the way we love ourselves by offering up our very *best* to our guests?

Jesus tells a story in Matthew 25 about what will happen when he returns to earth in his glory. He says he will separate people into two categories, onto to his right and his left. He commends those on his right, saying

> *'For I was hungry and you gave me something to eat,*
>
> *I was thirsty and you gave me something to drink,*
>
> *I was a stranger and you invited me in,*
>
> *I needed clothes and you clothed me,*
>
> *I was sick and you looked after me,*
>
> *I was in prison and you came to visit me.'*
>
> —Matthew 25:35-36

I read this passage recently and realized that was a pretty good working definition for the kind of hospitality we are talking about in this chapter. They "offered food and drink, they invited in, they clothed, they looked after, and they visited."

These people on his right were confused and asked God, "Wait, when did that ever happen?" Jesus replied,

> *"Whatever you did for one of the least of these brothers and sisters of mine, you did for me."*

The whole process is repeated for those on the left, except Jesus condemns these people because they did *not* feed him, offer him a drink, clothe him, visit him, or take him in.

They are also confused.

> *"Lord, when did we see you hungry or thirsty or a stranger or needing clothes or sick or in prison and did not help you?"*

The panic is practically palpable. "Whoa, whoa! We totally would have! That's exactly what we were waiting for!"

Jesus simply replies that whatever they did not do for one of the least of these, they did not do for him.

I think the group that did not feed, clothe, or visit, may have been waiting for a *radical* opportunity. They were waiting, maybe, for Jesus himself to appear on their doorstep. It seems as though they did not even see the opportunities to practice hospitality that were in front of them. These opportunities didn't seem big enough, maybe. They didn't seem important enough, radical enough.

Let us not neglect real opportunities to feed and clothe, to visit and to welcome those around us. Be radical. But do not let your radness be an excuse for inhospitality. Sometimes asking the question, "What is the best we can do?" is paralyzing. It might stop all action until a satisfactory, committee-approved and budget-approved, vetted answer can be found.

Do *something* in the meantime, while you're working towards your best.

Your children are watching. Be both radical *and* real with the least of these. (And just to be safe, do it with the greatest too. They might not be as great as they think they are.) In doing so, you will be serving none other than Jesus, in your midst.

DO *SOMETHING* IN THE MEANTIME, WHILE YOU'RE WORKING TOWARDS YOUR BEST.

In a nutshell:

Practice radical and real hospitality in your home.

8. DON'T MAKE PROMISES YOU CAN'T KEEP

#RichMelheim

It's common at the beginning of a summertime blockbuster action movie to have a scene where the hero makes a bold promise to someone. It usually plays out something like this. Movie opens to scenes of a typical family living a happy life. Then something terrible threatens peace in the galaxy. Now one of the parents must go on a journey to right this wrong in the world. The child cries out to parent: "Don't go!" Parent looks child in the eye and says in a gravelly voice, "I'm coming back for you. *I promise.*"

I always roll my eyes at that point.

I think, "You promise you're coming back? You're heading off to fight an army of alien invaders that has taken out half of the east coast cities, but *you're* going to be coming back alive? Because you *promise*?"

Maybe this would ruin the flow of the movie, but I wish they'd say something more like this: "I'm going to do everything in my power to come back for you. *But I want you to know that no matter what happens, I love you.*"

A lot of pain has been caused in the Christian culture because promises have been made in pulpits, songs, and Bible studies that should never have been made. Many of these promises sound something like this: "God wants you to be happy, so if you believe in him, your life will be amazing."

A LOT OF PAIN HAS BEEN CAUSED IN THE CHRISTIAN CULTURE BECAUSE PROMISES HAVE BEEN MADE IN PULPITS, SONGS, AND BIBLE STUDIES THAT SHOULD NEVER HAVE BEEN MADE.

If we tell these made-up promises to our children, they will likely trust us at first, because children can be very trusting. But eventually they will grow up. Their heads bump into things and their thoughts will too. In the storm of life, they will run for solid ground, and they may find the promises they heard as children seem to crumble beneath them.

It can be even more confusing when these promises seem to play out so perfectly for the PTA president, or our in-laws, or the pastor's son. *Why are their lives so perfect and yet mine is so filled with sorrow?*

Part of culture's deep distrust of religious culture is that many promises have been made that were disingenuous. *If you follow Jesus, your life will be better. If you tithe, you'll always have enough money. If you pray earnestly enough, then God will give you what you want. If you deserve it, God will heal you.* Some of these promises were made to specific people in the Bible, but they were not meant to be true for all people for all time. Some are principals that are generally true in life, but are not meant to be promises. And some have no root in scripture whatsoever.

We don't want to perpetuate that culture in any way by making it seem like these <18> experiences are a promise or a checklist that will guarantee a faith-filled or obedient child. They are not.

One of the best <18> experiences you can have with your kids is to not make promises to them that you can't keep.

Of course, I learned that lesson the hard way when my kids were toddlers and preschoolers. I learned that I had to be careful when I mention 'the park,' for example, or I'd have a crushed spirit to deal with when the errands took longer than expected and time ran out.

But that's not the kind of promise I'm talking about. What I'm talking about here is the importance of spiritual promises. Maybe we aren't outright *promising* something. Maybe we're just dropping lots of hints. Our words are very powerful in the minds of our children. It's worth taking a look at if we're implying any promises. Do we imply that if our kids go to church they'll be happier? Do we teach them that if they marry a Christian they'll have great sex, won't get divorced, and will live happily ever after? Do we give them the distinct impression Christian friends won't ever hurt them or talk behind their back?

Christians are flawed people just like everyone else. And God is pretty clear in the Bible that suffering is more common than not when we follow him. So let's not perpetuate a rosy picture of an easy, conflict-free life.

If we act like Mad Men, treating the gospel like a product we need to market, promising or implying that our urgent carnal desires will be fulfilled in Christendom, then, of course, the next generation will abandon ship when the seas become rocky. If you told them that as long as they stay in *this* ship, the sea will always be smooth, they will have no reason to stay when the sea proves to have storms.

Men's and women's brains are typically wired slightly differently. Women tend to have more connections between the halves of their brain, and because of this, women often think about issues in more complex ways. They are more easily able to see the connections and ramifications of an idea in multiple arenas. They see how *this* affects *that*, and they can process ideas on multiple levels. This is one reason they tend to be better at multitasking.

This means that it can be easy for mothers to immediately conjure up multiple worst-case scenarios to *any* given situation. This happens in a flash, without any effort. They can immediately tell their kids ten ways something could end badly. On one hand this has, undoubtedly, saved the lives of many children. On the other hand, this can create a lot of stress and worry in the life of an average mother.

Sometimes Arlyce would lay awake at night after we talked about a long, difficult decision. She'd be second-guessing it. She'd turn to me and say, "Can you guarantee me worst-case-scenario-number-five won't happen?"

"No," I'd say. "I can only guarantee you that I love you."

Her brow still furrowed, she'd ask, "Aren't you even *worried about it?*"

"No," I'd say. "That part of my brain isn't talking to the other part of my brain! Good night!"

We don't know what tomorrow will bring. We make the best decision we can today and adjust as needed tomorrow.

We can't even make our hearts beat. We don't make the sun rise. We don't decide how our boss will invest our company's retirement fund. We can't stand next to our children every moment and protect them from every danger. And even if we could do all of this, we can't stop time from marching on. There is so much you *can't* guarantee. If you march off to save the east coast cities from an alien invasion in a summer blockbuster movie, you're *not* going to be able to guarantee you'll come home.

Just guarantee your love through it all.

The Bible refers to the Holy Spirit as a deposit, a guarantee of our inheritance in heaven. That pretty much sums up what we know for sure that God promises us. In Jesus, God promises that we will inherit eternal life. Not because of our deeds, but because are adopted into God's family. And until that day, we have the Holy Spirit with us. God will not abandon us. God will be with us, strengthening and comforting us through it all. God's love is guaranteed to us. That is what we can promise to our children about God.

9. MODEL IT DAILY

Consider spiritual disciplines.

#RichMelheim

There are about seventy-times-seven-thousand books that you could read about the spiritual disciplines. Spiritual disciplines vary somewhat by denomination, but they are all basically practices intended to grow your spiritual maturity. Discipline refers to self-discipline, not punishments. It is like this: *Emily is lactose intolerant and she is disciplined enough to avoid dairy, even when the DQ opens for the summer. She knows a blizzard will just send her to the bathroom for the rest of the evening. Not worth it.*

That's maturity. That's discipline. It's really not anything so special or horrible or hard; it's simply growing up. Slowly, daily, gaining the wisdom, experience, and maturity that comes with age.

Of course, wisdom, experience, and maturity don't *necessarily* come with age. That's where discipline comes in. If I want to be a pillar of the community at my retirement party, I'm going to need to start now and slowly make a lifetime of small, mature choices.

What we gain from spiritual disciplines is something that happens slowly over time. Sometimes I make great leaps and bounds and feel alive in every verse I read and every prayer I pray. Sometimes I feel like there are steep mountains in front me, and every step I take is unstable. As often as not, I slip back down the side of the hill. But I keep going. That's discipline. Occasionally, I reach the top of a mountain and have the most amazing view. Sometimes I am able to say, "All of those crumbling steps were worth it." Sometimes I am able to say, "From up here I can finally see where I need to go next." Sometimes there is little clarity, but just another mountain ahead of me. So I just keep going.

When we do these things, we're not just doing it for ourselves. It's for the little eyes watching us too. When we think about the life skills that come easily to us, I'd bet many of them are things we watched our parents do. I'm not talking only about spiritual things, I'm talking about regular *life* things. Do we go to work on time? Do we exercise regularly? Do we know how to make healthy meals? Are the kitchen counters always cleaned off before we go to bed? Do we find cleaning the bathroom to be hell or just another task that needs to be done?

The things that we do without much effort are probably the things we saw our parents do during our most formative eighteen years.

I'm not saying it's impossible for an adult to gain life skills. People do it every day. But we have to spend a *long* time learning how to do these things in the natural, second-nature way that we are able to do the things we learned to do as a child.

When we see our parents do something as we grow up, we see how to do it in almost any kind of circumstance that comes up. Take exercise, for example. If I grew up with parents who exercised, I'd see how they did it through new babies, through vacations, through kids getting strep, through Mom getting strep, and then kids getting strep *again.* I'd see them continue through celebrations or through being mad at someone. I'd see when they took a day off and when they *didn't* take a day off. I'd see how much they loved it and how much they just did it anyway, even when they didn't *feel* like it.

So when I was faced with a bad day, I'd have a very clear picture in my mind of what to do. Words don't teach us these kind of things. People do. Not people's words. The people themselves.

The same thing is true of spiritual disciplines. Even very private disciplines come out in the intimacy of a home. Bob's wife Carol prays for people faithfully. She prays by herself and does not make a show out of it. But her kids would find prayer lists on her bedside stand. They knew she would be praying for their friends before they came over to her house.

It won't work if we do it just to get noticed by our kids. A side benefit of being authentic is that it has a positive impact on those we love. The reason to be authentic isn't to fool other people into doing something we want, though. That's obviously not authentic.

Here are a few of the spiritual disciplines and what they could look like:

Prayer.

Prayer is communicating with God.

It can be written lists you refer to throughout the day.

It can be sitting down to journal a prayer if you have a difficult time focusing on praying in your head.

It can be spoken aloud and with great feeling.

It can be whispered tentatively.

It can be public and it can be in community, but for our purposes here we will focus on personal prayer.

Prayer ought to be spoken in humility, not arrogance.

Prayer can be your own words.

You can pray psalms, the Lord's Prayer, or the prayers of the apostles, if you feel uncertain about how to start.

Prayer can make requests of God for yourself.

You can pray for those you know and those you don't know.

Prayer can be very honest.

You can pray about the temporal things, like food.

You can plead.

Prayers can simply praise God.

You can be thankful in your prayers when gratefulness is bubbling up naturally in your heart.

You can also be thankful in your prayers as a practice, by meditating on God's goodness in order to walk you slowly towards feeling thankful in the depths of your heart.

I have a friend who had a very difficult time during the year after her child was born. Sleep deprivation, financial difficulties, marriage tension, and no family or friends close by had put her in a place of deep sadness. She had heard in her Bible study about the importance of praying thankful prayers, so every day she began to write down a few things she was thankful for.

It felt so stiff and empty, she told me, to write things she knew she *should* be thankful for, but didn't actually *feel* thankful for them. But the practice slowly changed her perspective and gave her the security to keep moving forward in all of the problems she faced. Nothing quickly got fixed. *She* slowly changed.

Prayer can be in the morning when you first open your eyes before you get out of bed.

Prayer can be when you're trying to drift off to sleep.

Prayer can happen in the car during rush hour.

Prayer can be instigated by a calendar update reminder.

Prayer can happen in the hour of your greatest need, even if you've never uttered a word of it before. God welcomes you with open arms.

Prayer can be for impossible things.

It can be for very normal small things.

Prayer is communication with God.

Learning God's Word.

If you have not yet discovered the joy it is to study God's Word, then I am really quite excited for you.

"Thy Word is a lamp unto my feet," David writes in the Psalms.

The Word of God is a living resource, providing wisdom, insight, guidance, and comfort. It has widened my view of God and focused my view. It has brought me deep joy and deep conviction.

You don't have to know all of the original Greek and the historical context of a book in order to get something out of the scripture. Much of it is pretty straight forward.

Learning Bible verses is a fine place to start. When I was growing up, my mother had a small box shaped like a loaf of bread that she kept in the middle of our table. Inside the box were cards with Bible verses on them. On the outside of the box was written, "Our Daily Bread." We would read a scripture verse during most of our dinners.

As an adult at Faith Inkubators, I have created a similar resource—a list of 52 verses, one for each week of the year, that cover the breadth and depth of what God tells us in the Bible. It's not going to replace learning scripture as a whole, but it's a great place to start.

God's Word can be digested as bite-sized morsels and as entire meals.

When you sit down to study the Word of God in bigger sections, the book of John is a great place to start. Think of it like a documentary of Jesus' life while he was here on earth. Romans is a good book to read after that. It continually reminds you of God's gift of grace. You could try the book of Acts next. Acts is an account of the amazing adventures of the first Christians. After you've finished these books, you could read the whole New Testament.

Psalms and Proverbs can make wonderful daily devotionals to read—a Psalm or a verse or two from Proverbs each day.

To see the big picture of how it all fits together, you'll want to read the Old Testament, rich in history and stories of faith.

If you already know the depth of joy that awaits in his Word, and you struggle to find a way to incorporate it more regularly into your life, here are a few suggestions of things that have helped us.

Participate in a Bible study. The scriptures are a diverse body of work, written in many styles and with multiple historical contexts. Getting a little bit of context about a book of the Bible and walking through it with a teacher will give you a great jumping off point when you read it by yourself. Participating in a Bible study also helps because it gets you in the habit of going to the scriptures regularly.

Study an overview of scriptures. The books of the Bible aren't isolated stories. They work together as one body. Knowing how the books all fit together really helps.

Pray before you read. Pray that the Holy Spirit would reveal something to you as you read. Pray that you would understand the scriptures.

Use a journal. Bob keeps a notebook with him on all his travels. When he reads the scriptures, he writes down one or two things from the passage that stood out to him.

Be flexible to find what works for you. I have friends who use a phone app to remind them to read their daily scriptures. I have friends who read first thing in the morning, or last thing at night, or during their first morning break. If something doesn't seem to be working for you, try something new!

Other spiritual practices.

Fasting. Some people see fasting as a pretty extreme measure, but you can begin to fast, and even participate in fasts with your children, in a very manageable way. There are many reasons and ways to fast, but one thing God says in Isaiah is this:

> *"Is this not the kind of fasting I have chosen:*
>
> *To loose the chains of injustice*
>
> *And untie the cords of the yoke*
>
> *To set the oppressed free*
>
> *And break every yoke?*
>
> *Is it not to share your food with the hungry*
>
> *And to provide the poor wanderer with shelter—*
>
> *When you see the naked, to clothe them,*
>
> *And not to turn away from your own flesh and blood?"*
>
> —Isaiah 58:6-7

So one great way to fast is to use the time you would have spent on eating to remember and pray for those who don't have enough food to live, and to use the money you would have spent on food to give to those people.

I have friends who did a "rice fast" every Wednesday night with their kids during Lent. They just ate rice on

Wednesday night for dinner. It was a stark contrast to their normal meals, but it was still a meal. It was simple, but it was very memorable for the kids. They remembered that not everyone in the world has access to food, and they used the money they saved from those dinners to give to those in need. It was small. But small is a great way to start.

When their daughter grew up, she taught Sunday school and had her class participate in a rice fast for their snack time during Lent. She'd set up the rice cooker when they got to church in the morning and she dished out little cups of rice for each student during snack time. The kids actually loved it. When our whole bodies participate in something, we learn and process information in a much deeper way. When Easter came, she brought in a "feast" of fruits, vegetables, and cookies—after a long season of plain rice for snack time, the feast was a visceral reminder of the kind of life Jesus offers us.

Rest can also be spiritual practice. Rest is ordered actually in the Ten Commandments. We are to keep the Sabbath Day holy and do no work on it, since God rested on the seventh day. I mention it here because spiritual disciplines can easily seem like long lists of things we do to impress God.

When we take one day out of the week to rest, we are almost literally putting our life in God's hands. There are important things that we *need* to do. We probably don't have time to stop working for one day. This day doesn't have to be Saturday or Sunday, but spending one whole day each week to worship God and rest is a practice that reminds us that we are not gods. Rather, we are God's.

None of these disciplines are things we *have* to do. They are things we have loved and gained so much from in our lives. We recommend them because we have found them to be helpful. They are things that have brought us closer to Jesus.

Wait, scratch that. That's not the best way to put it.

Jesus is already close to all of us. In fact, our bodies are the temple of the Holy Spirit. God has made a *home* in us. The Holy Spirit is with us to stay. Rather, these are things that have helped us to "grow into the full measure of Christ." They have helped us mature.

In a nutshell:

Spiritual disciplines, like prayer, reading the Bible, fasting, and keeping the Sabbath are valuable tools that can help you and your children mature in Christ.

10. THE NEAREST EXIT MAY BE BEHIND YOU

#BobLong

I was seated on a flight from Green Bay to Minneapolis in the front row of the coach cabin. The doors were on our left, and a fantastic aisle in front of me made for lots of leg room. I'm six foot five, so I was really happy to get this seat.

The flight attendant had a seat that folded down right in front of me which she used during take-off and landing. Flight attendants and public speakers both tend to be pretty extroverted, so we talked the entire flight. Plane conversations can go the way of football scores (especially when you're flying into or out of Green Bay), but occasionally the conversations will cover something even more important than the playoff standings.

On this particular day, the flight attendant told me *everything* about her life. As we departed from Green Bay our conversation began with seemingly lightweight information. *"I have three kids…"* But her eyes filled with tears as she unfolded more of her story while our plane rose to altitude. By the time we hit thirty thousand feet, she was telling me, *"I thought I couldn't have any babies...*" Her voice was catching in her throat. I hadn't responded to her yet—she was still in the middle of her story—when we heard the *bing* of the seatbelt light turning off. She picked up the microphone, blinked her eyes dry in one blink, and clicked on the microphone. She was instantly calm and assertive, "*The captain has turned off the seatbelt sign.*" Her professional voice had taken over, projecting confidence and pleasantness.

I stared at her in amazement. This voice that sounded joyful and calm was a completely different voice than the one she was using less than one minute ago, which sounded so raw and real. She reminded us calmly to keep our seatbelts on while we are seated, in case of any unforeseen turbulence.

I don't want that to happen to my voice when I talk about Jesus, I thought.

I DON'T WANT THAT TO HAPPEN TO MY VOICE WHEN I TALK ABOUT JESUS, I THOUGHT.

She became a performer in that moment. Now, don't get me wrong. That's *totally* appropriate for a flight attendant at cruising altitude while speaking over the intercom. You don't want to hear your flight attendant choking down tears while she is reminding you that *the nearest exits may be behind you.*

But when we share about what Jesus has done in our lives, let's not sound distant and professional, like we're announcing it over an intercom. Let's share it like we are knee-to-knee across an aisle, having an actual conversation. Like we are in the same boat, or on the same flight. I don't want spiritual accents. It's got to be the body and the spirit; it's got to be all of us. It should not be a memorized presentation that we give.

Jesus didn't become a human in order to give us a presentation. The Bible is not meant to be an in-flight safety video. That might be how we're using it now, but that's not how it originated. It is a collection of stories of real human lives. It's poetry written in choking voices and through eyes brimming with tears. It's research from a doctor, who carefully interviewed those who had first-hand interactions with Jesus while he was on earth. The Bible is the account of what Jesus did, what he spoke, and how he listened when he was knee-to-knee with mankind. The Bible is letters written from prisons to dearly loved friends. That is the way in which God's Word has been conveyed to us. In this very *real life* way. Let's not turn that raw story into a rote script we deliver with blank eyes and smiles. Let's tell it the way it's meant to be told.

Let's talk about real life, and rejoice with those who rejoice, weep with those who weep. Truth without love is brutality, and love without truth is compromise. That's why we need to speak the truth in love, but love assumes and requires a relationship.

Paul says, "We loved you so much that we shared with you not only God's Good News but our own lives." (1 Thess. 2:8b, NLT)

Wait a minute, I thought that's all we need to give people. Just God's Word.

Paul said, "Just as a nursing mother cares for her children, so we cared for you." (1 Thess. 2:7b-8a)

Paul spoke truth in love in the context of relationship. Our spirituality shouldn't be sectioned off to Sunday mornings or to certain ways of speaking. Our spirituality should be woven through all of our life and in all of our relationships.

In a nutshell:

Speak from the heart. Converse knee-to-knee, using our unscripted, everyday voice.

11. IMMERSE YOURSELF IN A SERVANT EXPERIENCE

#RichMelheim

Serving our communities is one of the most life-shaping experiences we can have with our kids. That makes sense, of course. Meaningful service is actually one of the most attractive things our faith has to offer the next generation. They *want* to make a difference, and the more we connect them to Christians who are doing real good in the world, the more real and meaningful this faith is. The more we put our money where our mouth is, the more weight our words will have.

There are many ways we can dip our toes into the water of serving together, right in our own backyard. We could serve in **our families, our churches, our communities, and our world.**

In Our Families

Clearing the table and doing the dishes together, or spending a Saturday tending a garden, may feel so small it's not worth noting. But these small recurring activities can impress upon our kids that we value a life of service.

These simple actions can feel endless or thankless. *The dishes are dirty, again?* But these small tasks at home are where we can model an attitude of service. We serve each other because we are serving God. We don't keep score and we don't grumble. We all do our part (even though sometimes life isn't fair).

I know a few friends who keep a set of unbreakable dishes in a low cupboard so that even her littlest kids can help set the table.

When we set an example of service in our own families, and when we ask our children to join us in these tasks, we put our faith into action in a meaningful and memorable way.

In Our Churches

There are likely ways that our families can serve together in our own churches. Perhaps kids can help parents at the welcome desk, or tweens can help in the nursery. Perhaps they can hand out bulletins. Older teens could be trained to monitor the soundboard or run a video camera. I know of a church where a grade school student was one of the regular drummers for their Sunday morning worship team. He might not have been the best drummer in the world, but I think that might have been some of the most beautiful worship music I have ever heard.

Incorporating our kids into the fabric of our church gives them value and provides a way for them to connect meaningfully. It also gives them a realistic picture of how the world works. Church isn't just a place we go to *get* things. It is a family where all members contribute to the care, support, and survival of the family.

In Our Communities

I think sometimes we mistakenly believe that our service is only for God when it is done in a Christian setting. Any time we serve the people God created, it is an offering to God.

Most of our communities have a number of opportunities for people to volunteer, and many of them would welcome children to serve with parents—libraries, recycling centers, sports programs, or homeless shelters all rely on help from people just like you. This could even be a great way to serve God through our passions or through our children's passions.

Thanksgiving is a time when many shelters provide a special meal for their guests, and they are often looking for a lot of volunteers at that time. Many times the meal is not even on Thanksgiving Day, so it doesn't even have to interrupt a traditional family gathering. Most organizations do a pretty good job of making volunteering on that day accessible to new people. It could make a great yearly tradition.

In Our World

#BobLenz

One of the most memorable ways to serve together is to go on a cross-cultural service trip. Some churches will send a youth group or a group of adults to another country to participate in a service project (perhaps to build a school or lead a summer camp). These are often life-changing experiences for a family.

When we participate in international or cross-cultural trips like this, it's important to make sure that we're partnering with local people and listening to their needs. In fact, one of the most life-changing parts of these trips is getting to meet and to learn from the amazing local people.

"DO YOU THINK YOU BROUGHT JESUS HERE WITH YOU IN YOUR SUITCASE? DID YOU NOT THINK HE WAS HERE IN OUR CULTURE AND IN OUR SONGS, IN OUR DANCE, AND EVEN IN SOME OF OUR PRACTICES? ALL YOU NEED TO DO IS POINT OUT JESUS TO MY PEOPLE. HE IS ALREADY HERE. YOU AND I JUST NEED TO BE A TOUR GUIDE AND POINT HIM OUT."

One of the reasons Compassion International has such a successful child sponsorship program is because when they go into a city or village, they run the program through local people in an already established local church. In each community, the sponsorship programs look a little bit different, based on the local needs and culture. Compassion doesn't send in Americans to decide what it should look like. They partner with local people.

I visited my friend, Sunitha, in India. I was doing some outreach events there, preaching the Good News. As we walked around one afternoon, she asked me, "Do you think you brought Jesus here with you in your suitcase? Did you not think he was here in our culture and in our songs, in our dance, and even in some of our practices? All you need to do is point out Jesus to my people. He is already here. You and I just need to be a tour guide and point him out."

I visit Alaska every year to do school assemblies in schools in the bush villages. Bush villages can only be reached by plane or by boat. In many of these villages, the populations are mostly indigenous peoples. Every time I get to go there, I'm in awe of the reflection of God in their people and their land.

In many of the houses, you'll see a large baleen—a blue whale's tooth—though it's not really a tooth like we think of a tooth. Its makeup is more like a bristle, and it looks more like an enormous feather. The baleen hanging above the doorpost or on the wall is often significantly taller than I am. The whales use them, not to bite anything, but to strain the water. They open their mouths to fill them with ocean water, then close them, pushing out water between their baleen, and keeping the tiny krill inside so they can eat them. I talked to one of my hosts about it, and he explained what it was. "Isn't it amazing," he said, "that one of the world's largest creatures eats one of the smallest?"

Yes, amazing. God has created this world with such intricate details. These villages have a front row seat to God's majesty. The respect they have for God's creation is quite inspiring to me.

When I go to the schools, I notice that in every lunchroom they have pictures of all the elders in that village prominently displayed on the walls. One day an elder came to visit the school and the students all crowded around her like she was a celebrity.

There are reflections of God in these people and in their land that astound me. These trips are not a charity I do. They are an exchange of gifts between God's people. One of the pastors who brings me up there, though, knows the deep love I have for fishing and for nature, and he has told me, "Bob, I know that you come here for our students and not for yourself, because you've never come up here during fishing seasons." Even without fishing, even in the shortest days of winter, even with all the struggles in the villages (just like my own town, and my own people), they brightly reflect God's glory.

One of the villages, Cold Bay, is a bit of a hub for the region. The airport there has a longer runway than many of the others. There was a missionary, Bill, who came to this town decades ago to tell them about Jesus. The local village told him outright, "You are welcome to stay here with us, but we will not listen to what you have to say until you die here. You are not one of us, until you die here."

I heard that and thought, *Yikes!* That seems like a catch-22. How can you tell them about Jesus after you're dead?

This missionary was not fazed a bit. He lived there his entire life, raising a family, growing into old age and then dying among them. He saw not one single neighbor come to know Jesus.

After his death, they did listen to him. Today there are many Christians in that town. The missionary's children stayed and lived there, for it was their home now too. One is a schoolteacher, one is a judge, and one is a nurse. They belong to the community now, in a way they never could have if their father had just seen the village as a group of potential converts instead of neighbors. Humans just like him.

We don't want to limit our thinking of service to the realm of "events." We don't want to think about doing service only during a two-week trip, and then the rest of the time we think about ourselves.

Whether we live in a village in Alaska or in a suburb of Cleveland, our lives are telling daily about what we believe. Like Bill, the missionary in Alaska, we must understand that this isn't a two-week job. It's not a year or two out of your life. It's not even the eighteen years your kids are at home. It's a lifelong journey.

I think most people hold a belief similar to the people of Cold Bay. *We won't believe what you have to say unless you're willing to give your life for it.* Giving up your life doesn't necessarily mean you have to die. There are so many ways to give our lives. The slow, daily giving of our life for a cause, or for the benefit of someone else, is the way most of us will give our lives away.

It's not just teenagers whose lives can be positively impacted by going on a servant event. I have heard of a church that intentionally brings along two or three people who are not Christians on their mission trips. Their church often goes to build structures, so they'll find people and bring them specifically because of their skills in plumbing or carpentry. As often as not, these lives are changed when they work side by side with those who are giving their entire lives because Jesus poured out his life for them.

We have, perhaps, overlooked the most appealing front door to our church: welcoming unbelievers to join us in acts of real service to our communities and to the world.

Our friend, Bill Oeschler, actually had the course of his life changed on a service trip to Ecuador. He was not a believer when he first met and married his wife. A few years after their marriage, she asked him, "When are you going to start investigating what I believe?"

He said, "What are you talking about?"

"You told me before we got married, that you would investigate what I believed," she reminded him.

"I don't remember this at all," he brazenly admitted, which led to what he called *a huge fight*.

Eventually, he discovered that he just could not defend his spiritual philosophy. He told her that as long as she could find a church he was comfortable in, they could go. They found one that met in a junior high gym. They sat in folding chairs and wore jeans. Bill said he'd have gone barefoot if he could have. That was his style. The worship leader played contemporary music on a Casio keyboard.

Bill had been given *The Way* when he was a kid, a Bible that was intended to be an easy read. He tried to read it the way he would read any other book: starting at the beginning. By the time he got to the long list that read, "Someone begat somebody else," he put it down and never picked it up again.

At this time, his wife brought him another Bible. One night at three in the morning he was sitting in his living room, unable to sleep. He thought, "What should I read? Shirley McLain? A little Steven King?" He lived in literature. He had books on the wall behind him, books in front of him on a shelf. His den was lined with books. As he pondered what to read in the middle of the night, he saw in front his brand new, never opened Scofield Bible, sitting on his coffee table.

He picked it up and his finger dropped to John 3:16.

He had *no idea*, he earnestly reminded us, about how the Bible worked. He had no context for chapter and verse, but he did remember seeing John 3:16 on a football game or something. He read the verse.

> *"For God loved the world so much that he gave his only Son so that anyone who believes in him shall not perish but have eternal life."*
>
> —John 3:16 (TLB)

He just sat there and thought, "Well, it's either all true, or it's all not." And then he just decided it was all true. He received Jesus on the porch of their music director's house at the next small group meeting. He got a call a few days after that from his pastor, who said, "Hey, we're going on a mission trip to Ecuador. We'd love for you to come with us."

"Oh, not me. I'm the guy who just, you know, told my story in church last week." He'd just given his testimony, but he didn't even know the church word for it.

"No, you're perfect," his pastor said.

That trip changed the course of his life. They were up in the mountains working with the Quechua people. He thought, "This is faith, putting your life on the line."

The course of his life changed when he came home. He quit his job, and they both went back to school. Bill headed up marketing for Zondervan, where he worked on the production of The Bible Experience, an audio production of the Bible read by four hundred of the best black actors and actresses. Before that, he helped with the End of the Spear films, a real story about missionaries in Ecuador. Interestingly, he had met Rachel Saint on that life-changing trip to Ecuador. Rachel was a key person in the End of the Spear stories, but he didn't know who she was or anything about her history at that time.

If we want our young people, and our new believers, to have any reason to remain in their faith, there must be something worth staying for. If belief in God is a Sunday morning event, junior high gymnasiums and Cassio keyboards are going to get old eventually. DJs in the lobby and light shows and video production are not going to convince people Jesus is relevant to their lives.

Going on an eye-opening, multi-cultural experience, where we see first-hand Christians putting their lives on the line for their faith, can make a deep impression on our lives. We can see that, in fact, when we lose our life, we do find it. This can give us the perspective to come home and re-order our priorities in our own neighborhoods. We can lay down our lives here by thinking not of ourselves first, but thinking of others. Most of the world is telling us to look out for ourselves. It helps to have had first-hand experience of looking in the eyes of people who are giving away their entire life, and realizing they are the happiest people we know. It helps to have first-hand experience in giving and finding that it is in giving that we receive.

#RichMelheim

Life-changing service trips don't just have to be across culture boundaries. These big events or trips can happen within our own communities too.

When I first became a youth pastor, I was young and abounding with energy. We had a great youth group. People looked out for each other. I was someone they came to talk to. Our church supported us. It was a glorious few years.

And then two tragedies struck our community. Over the course of a few months, two of our recently graduated high school students committed suicide.

Our entire community reeled from these events. Our youth group, the little flock of adolescent sheep I was charged with guiding, found these two deaths unfathomable. These were their mentors, their big brothers, their heroes. How could this have happened?

I didn't really know what to do. I wrote a play. That summer our youth group took a long road trip from Minnesota to California and back, to perform this play about suicide. They spent their summer on a mission trip to America, to tell other churches and communities that suicide is something we should not ignore. They performed a play as a way to start conversations and prevent tragedies.

Unbeknownst to them, it was a summer-long therapy session. A way to slowly process, every night and across state lines, in front of strangers and with their closest friends, this confusing thing had happened in their midst.

It was a ministry they gave, and it was a ministry they received.

I do a lot of work with AJ the Animated Illusionist. He is part of the World's Greatest Magic Show in Vegas, the number one family show for three years in a row. He performs at some of the biggest venues all over the world.

My mom passed away a few years ago, and she wanted the message of life that she lived out in her radical hospitality to come out at her funeral, because faith comes from hearing. So we had AJ perform one of his acts, called, "From Birth to Death." We had to group some Sunday school benches together so he could stand on top of them for his act. It is a two-minute presentation of the gospel from creation to death and resurrection. Afterward, he allowed people to respond. Over two hundred people received Christ into their heart at my mom's funeral.

I have another friend, Donna, who had a small wedding a few years ago. By small, I mean there were just a few dozen of us attending. In other ways it was one of the "biggest" wedding events that I have ever attended. The wedding was a multi-day event in Vegas. They pulled out all the stops. After a four-star meal, they moved us into another room for a surprise. They brought in a Michael Jackson impersonator to do a private show just for us! He was incredible. He must have had plastic surgery because he looked *just like him. Then* they gave everyone a ticket to one of the biggest shows in Vegas!

The favors they gave us really put to shame the little bag of Jordan Almonds we gave out at our wedding. They had filled huge gift baskets and written a note that said, "This is the stuff that means the most to us and we want to share it with you." It included a CD with both Christian and non-Christian songs, their favorite chocolate bars, the best local honey, and a copy of my book, *Grace*.

So there was *Grace*, intermingling with local honey and Elvis impersonators in Vegas. Where Grace belongs, I think. God's Grace doesn't belong on a shelf.

God doesn't want another AJ. He doesn't want another Bob, or even a Bob impersonator. He *definitely* doesn't want you to get plastic surgery to look more like me.

He wants you to be you. What do you do? It probably wouldn't make sense for you to set up a stage and mime at a funeral. You might not be able to make huge gift baskets for all of the guests at your wedding.

But what could you do at your wedding? Your anniversary party? An end of the year picnic? Birthday? Family reunion?

What blessings could you share at a graduation party? What record of God's care could you include in a baby's "first year" book?

What would I want my friends to know more than anything else about this God of mine? How can we share it tastefully? That is to say: deliciously and respectfully? How can these special occasions be a testimony of what matters most in our lives?

"The tongue of the wise makes knowledge acceptable," Proverbs 15:2 (NASB). I'm not suggesting compromising what we believe. If we compromise, it's not truth. I think we can find a way to bring God's truth into our weddings and funerals, and the most important events in our families' lives.

We can still celebrate or grieve during these times.

In fact, Jesus was upset with the people who didn't dance enough at weddings and didn't cry enough at funerals.

> "We played the pipe for you
>
> and you did not dance.
>
> We sang a dirge
>
> And you did not cry."
>
> —Luke 7:32

We are definitely encouraged by God to embrace the full reality of what each of these events is intended to be. The beauty of God is that he is able to be there with us in all of those places. We can incorporate God's love into our celebrations and sorrows.

Ceremonies can be opportunities to share our hearts. It might not be in our Google Calendar to-do list, but it is OK if we put it there. We can meet God in our highs and our lows, and even in our celebrations and remembrances.

In a nutshell:

Share the Good News tastefully at big life events.

15. WHEN NECESSARY USE WORDS

#BobLenz

When I was 17, Rog and Pat Hermsen were the leaders at a retreat that we called TEC, or Teens Encounter Christ. It was at that retreat where I had my first real heart encounter with Jesus. Pat asked me to speak at the event the following weekend. I scratched down my thoughts in a notebook one night. I came to Pat the next day and threw the paper down in disgust.

"I know what to say, but I'm not living it," I said, frustration welling up inside me.

"Well," Pat said calmly, "maybe it's time to start."

"WELL," PAT SAID CALMLY, "MAYBE IT'S TIME TO START."

Those words from Pat made me realize I don't have to be perfect. I can simply start living it.

It might sound like a small thing, but those words were very pivotal for me. That is the kind of life I want for people—not just that they receive meaningful words, but that they give them too.

We are so aware at this moment in history that there are a lot of hypocrites out there. We hate hypocrites. Those ugly people who say one thing and then do something else with the way they live.

We have such a distaste for hypocrisy, though, that it has made us afraid to say much of anything. We don't want to be wrong, to hurt someone, or be *a hypocrite*.

But I don't want to live the safe life. I want to be like Pat who took a risk of being misunderstood by a football-player-sized, floppy-hair teen. I want to kindly, gently call people towards something more.

If I want to do what Rog and Pat did for me, what would that look like?

Well, one option is that I could hang around youth until someone threw down a notebook and said, "I know what to say, but I'm not living it."

Then I'd be ready with a Fast and Furious Soundtrack on cue and in my best deep movie-trailer voice, I'd speak the life-altering words:

"*Well, maybe it's time to start.*"

I can see it all now! We could create a curriculum where we study one word each week. On the last week, when we study the word "S*tart*" we give everyone who has attended a graduation certificate. We sell t-shirts that say *Start* and have *Start* conferences.

Of course, that would be focusing on entirely the wrong thing. The Japanese poet Matsuo Basho puts it this way:

"Do not seek to follow in the footsteps of the masters. Seek what they sought."[10]

I should not try to copy Pat's exact words, but I should try to follow in her footsteps, using words as one of the tools in my tool belt to call God's people into the full life God wants us to experience.

The words Pat spoke to me were not magic words. They were part of my personal journey, words connected to my past and a conduit to my future. Many things had brought me to that point in my life. I had witnessed my parents' day-in-day-out faith, I had seen how Pat and Rog live, I trusted Jesus at a youth camp, and I had just been working out on paper what I would tell young people about following Jesus.

In all of those things the Holy Spirit was shining a spotlight on my life that very day. I knew these things in my head, and I experienced them in my heart, but the blood was not making its way to my extremities. My hands and my feet were still asleep.

Her gentle but firm voice called to me, echoing the ancient psalm: *Wake up, oh sleeper.*

The words Pat spoke to me were not magic words, but they were still words.

I think the concern over making sure our words aren't misunderstood by someone can cause us to keep quiet too often. It's easy to feel like you don't know what to say, especially when it comes to talking about Jesus to people who don't know God's love yet. We don't want to harm and we don't want to be hypocritical. Those are all good desires. Sometimes it's best to listen. Most of the time it's best to choose your words carefully. But it's not always best to stay silent.

Jesus wanted the actions and the words to match. If our actions speak of the love of Christ but our words don't, that's also being hypocritical.

I know that my wife Carol wants me to show my love in my actions, but if I *never* spoke about it, well, we wouldn't even be married in the first place, I suppose. I might still be waiting by myself at the altar, wondering why she didn't understand from how I was acting that I wanted to marry her.

Pat's words to me that day on the retreat were truthful, firm words, but they were spoken kindly. If Pat had, instead, turned to me with daggers in her eyes and a cackling laugh and said, "Oh, I *know* you're not living it. That's obvious. What a disappointment you are."

That would have had a *very* different impact on my life.

When I was in high school, I was a bit of trouble. Once you are a bit of trouble in high school, it's easy to become a lot of trouble. You start to become known for the little things you do instead of for the person you are.

Most of my teachers thought I was no good. They would say to me in a superior way, "Oh, we've heard about you." They would make my friend, Chris Mitten and I sit in opposite corners of the classroom. Come on, how much trouble could we cause with just pencils and papers?

I took a Home Economics class one year. Just imagine all the trouble we could have caused in a class filled with electric mixers, hot ovens, and raw ingredients! But instead of separating us, teacher Pam Olson looked at us when we walked into her class and said gently, "I've heard about you, but I personally think there is a side of you those other teachers have never seen."

Sherry Simon, my gym teacher, wrote in my yearbook, "I don't think you're all trouble. I think you could change the world."

I tell you their names because I *remember* their names and I remember their *words*. I still think about these words, in fact. Imagine that! Thirty years later and the kind words from two high school teachers still lift me up.

SHE HEARD ME AND SHE RESPONDED IN LOVE. THAT'S REALLY THE BEST WAY TO USE OUR WORDS.

Be someone whose name is remembered. Not by top ten charts and history books, but in diaries and yearbooks and family stories. Be someone who could change the world, as Sherry Simon would say.

The words Pat spoke to me were specific words, spoken to me.

Pat knew me.

Pat listened to what I was saying.

She heard me and she responded in love. That's really the best way to use our words.

In a nutshell:

Don't shy away from using words, in love, to speak God's truth.

16. VALUE PEOPLE OVER THINGS

#RichMelheim

When I was growing up, we lived in a two-story house in a small town on the flat prairie of North Dakota. My sister and I each had a bedroom at either side of the top of the stairs on the second story. My mother would sit on the top step between our rooms and read books to us while we lay in our beds in the dark quiet nights. The soft light would float into our rooms from the hallway and we had to lay very still in order to hear Mom's voice.

When we were in grade school she read chapter books to us. She had been a teacher before we were born and she approached motherhood as an educator. I think these evenings were highlights for her, as they were for us. One of my favorite authors was Astrid Lindgren. I had a Pippi Longstocking kind of philosophy in life. *"Everything's going to work out." "Don't worry about me. I'll always come out on top."*

Astrid's story *Pippi Longstocking* resonated with me.

"Resonate" comes from "resound." To re-sound is to *sound again*. To hear again. It resonates in me and with me because it is familiar to me.

"RESONATE" COMES FROM "RESOUND." TO RE-SOUND IS TO *SOUND AGAIN*. TO HEAR AGAIN. IT RESONATES IN ME AND WITH ME BECAUSE IT IS FAMILIAR TO ME.

Maybe it resonated with me because my mom seemed to have a Pippi Longstocking philosophy. We were by no means rich, living on the single salary of a country parish pastor. But my parents always put a little money in the cupboard next to the refrigerator.

Mom would say to me, "If you need something there's always something there. But you know you got sisters, Richy. So don't just take it all. But you know there will always be enough."

She was always so affirming to me. If someone did something bad to me at school, she would say, "Oh, they must have had a bad day. I wonder what's hurting them so bad that they'd treat you like that, Richy dear." Or she'd say, "Maybe it was just a misunderstanding." In the house where I grew up, there was always enough room to extend grace to someone.

There was always enough in the cupboards. There was always enough in the fridge. This was not because we had scads of money, though. I know my parents' careful allotment of their resources was crucial. But I think this deep feeling of fullness in our house was due to the things that my parents valued.

Money was not their most valuable resource. Time was.

Money you can make, but you cannot make time. It is much too valuable of a resource to ever be *spent.* Don't spend your time. Invest your time.

My dad always invested time in me. He would leave the office to come see my baseball game or the play I was in. He had many things that required his time and wasn't able to give us every moment. There were many nights when he had meetings to attend, and he wouldn't be home at bedtime.

He tried, when he could, to turn even those commitments into ways to spend time with us. During Lent, Lutheran churches held evening services on Wednesdays. The churches near him agreed to do a pulpit exchange for those Wednesday nights. It meant a long drive through the prairie to another small town church, but, he told me with a twinkle in his eye, "If you travel to speak, you only need one good sermon!"

I would go with him on Wednesdays, leaving after school, listening to my dad preach in a new church. Then we'd drive home, and I'd fall asleep under the stars next to my dad as he drove us home in the car. Those are some of my favorite memories.

When we drove around town, if we ever came across any kind of new construction, Dad would pull off the road immediately and we'd walk past the ditch onto the building, looking at the bare structure. My dad would ask, "What do you think it's going to be? What do you think this room is? If this was your house where you would want your bedroom to be?"

It's quite powerful to have your dad ask you, "What do *you* think?"

Memories accrue in value over time. Even things we thought were cheesy as kids, or the horrible experience on vacation when we had a flat tire and had to stand in the pouring rain for an hour waiting for a tow truck. These memories age well. They gain value and become dearer to us over time. We love to recall and retell them.

Things, on the other hand, lose excitement over time. Even a long-awaited toy will soon lose its shimmer. A new toy is often quickly abandoned. A new smart phone becomes mundane.

But that's not how it is with memories. Memories become better with time.

Bob's kids used to travel with him during the summers. They told me that they tease him now about all of the "once in a lifetime opportunities" they experienced.

Bob would say, "Guys, this is a once in a lifetime opportunity to see Yellowstone!"

It was a "once in a lifetime opportunity" no less than four times over the course of their childhood. They drove out of their way for hours so they could stand on the four corners. "It's a once in a lifetime opportunity!" he explained.

Twice.

Bob's enthusiasm for the beauty of nature is unquenchable. His daughter told me that he was constantly pulling over to the side of the road, and they'd all pile out of the car to admire the sunset. Rather, the kids would all stand there sleepily while Bob was admiring the sunset. As often as not, it would bring tears to his eyes.

They were in Hawaii together just last year. Carol, Joyel and her husband were all sitting inside because there had just been a giant thunderstorm. Bob came running into the room. "You guys! You *have* to come see this! It's a double rainbow!" He dragged them all outside.

"Like we've never seen a double rainbow before!" Joyel told me later.

But she was laughing as she said it.

These memories turn into treasures. Whether your dad is moved by every sunset or the sight of new construction, even these quirks become treasures. You can become rich when these regular stones turn to gold over time in our memories.

My friend has an uncle who used to tell her, "Buy your kids one Christmas present, and then play *with* them. That's what they really want: time with you."

It might seem like a small thing to take <18> minutes every night to shut off your phone and look directly into the eyes of your kids and listen to them, without rushing to finish their often frustratingly incomplete and sometimes misinformed sentences. It is no small thing. If they grow up thinking they are worth the full attention of someone, it will shape the course of their lives.

Ideally, we spend lots of <18>s with our kids. <18> after they get home from school. <18> over breakfast. <18> on the commute. <18> if we can find a way for them to join us in a task at work, or a task in our work at home. <18> when we share our greatest joy with them, even if they roll their eyes. <18> when we support their interests, even if they confuse us.

Let's invest all of the <18>s we can.

In a nutshell:

Prioritize investing your time with your people over investing your money in things.

17. ASK A LOT OF QUESTIONS

#RichMelheim

I love Psalm 19.

> "The heavens declare the glory of God;
> the skies proclaim the work of his hands.
>
> Day after day they pour forth speech;
> night after night they reveal knowledge.
>
> They have no speech, they use no words;
> no sound is heard from them.
>
> Yet their voice goes out into all the earth,
> their words to the ends of the world."

If you are looking for God, you are going to find evidence everywhere. You'll find evidence if you look into a microscope, at the tiny world that exists in an individual cell.

A mitochondria is like a little energy factory inside each of our 100 trillion cells, taking in fat, sugar and protein, combining it with oxygen to provide just the right amount of energy it needs. Mitochondria break apart 2,000,000 different proteins into 47,000 enzymes and put them back into perfect combinations to give us exactly what we need. Look inside this miracle factory and you'll see something amazing. It's like tiny little trucks come into a factory with raw materials. The factory builds the chemicals to order, and the finished products are carried out to where they are needed, along with the energy to run them!

IF THERE IS NO GOD, THEN THIS WORLD IS REALLY A MIRACLE.

And think of bleeding. The moment you cut yourself, the skin gives a message, "Danger! I need prothrombin or I'm going to bleed out and get infected!" The factories kick in making the chemicals needed. Prothrombin dumps into the blood stream and mixes with plasma to create a mesh (thromboplastin) in and around the wound to clot the spot. At the same time, the chemical factories dump just the right chemicals into the blood and rush to the spot to kill the invading bacteria! The mesh is built. The anti-bacterial chemicals are delivered to the spot, the scab appears. The bacteria gets eaten up and flushed away. How did that happen? Impossible!

Forty-seven thousand chemicals being developed inside mini-factories inside every cell in your body? It's impossible. Blood clotting and eating up the invading bacteria on the spot? Impossible. If there is no God, then this world is really a miracle.

You can see God by zooming out, looking at the big picture on a macro level. Astrophysicist Dr. Hugh Ross could tell you about the moment of the Big Bang (or "*Then there was light,*" in my terminology). At that moment, there was a precision that was mathematically, statistically impossible within microseconds of the explosion. First, there was nothing, then there was everything.

Before the Big Bang, there was no mass, energy, time, or space. Think about that. The moment before the moment, there was no moment. And then there was everything. If that explosion had happened at a microsecond of a different scale, there would be no element lighter than lead in the universe. If it had happened a microsecond off the other way, there would have been no item heavier than hydrogen and helium. This amazing world is all impossible.

There are really only two laws of physics: *nothing comes from nothing* and *something did.*

What do you want to call that something?

What if you were sitting with your friends, and you decided: *I'm just going to ask a lot of questions.* Grandma used to say that you catch a lot more flies with honey than you do vinegar. So instead of pounding the Bible down their throats, you just decide to ask questions.

You might ask, "How is this possible? Here is a cell and it has a factory that creates 47,000 enzymes and it knows when to design the exact right chemical for the exact right thing and turn it into usable energy."

"Here's this barrier between the brain and the blood that keeps out large molecules like bacteria and lets in exactly what the brain needs—oxygen and glucose to feed it. That's amazing. Here's this universe that is statistically impossible." You might ask, "How did that happen?"

It is amazing how life generates on Earth. Life needs a lot of oxygen but it can't have too much oxygen, because oxygen eats things up. It oxidizes. Like rust. That means the very first cells had to have a wall around them to protect them from too much oxygen. It means that the planet Earth had to have the perfect amount of ozone because if it didn't, UV lights would kill the cells.

So the cells had to have a cell wall before they had a cell, and they had to have a cell before they had a cell wall. *Wait, what?*

RNA are the instructions that tell DNA to build, and DNA are the instructions that tell RNA to build. So you had to have RNA before you had DNA, and you had to have DNA before you had RNA. That's just another way of saying, "Which came first, the chicken or the egg?" They both had to be first because you can't have one without the other. This whole universe is impossible.

The easiest way to share God's love with your friends is to know their highs and lows and care for them. Let the beauty of Jesus be seen in who you are and what you do. The second easiest way to share the Good News in a post-Christian culture is to simply ask a lot of questions. Conclusions you come to on your own are much more powerful than answers you are given. You don't have to be afraid of asking questions, or of any questions that our kids ask. As Psalm 19 says, "The heavens declare the glory of God." This is all crazy impossible, yet here it is. Wow! Isn't that interesting?

In a nutshell:

Ask questions. Don't just hand out answers.

18. BE A PRODIGAL PARENT

#BobLenz

My dad worked in a grocery warehouse when I was growing up. He worked from two in the afternoon to ten at night, five days a week, until he retired. He always had the weekends off, and we would head out of town as soon as we could Saturday morning to go hunting or fishing. That was his way of nurturing us.

We had beagles that would hunt rabbits. We had *really* good beagles. The beagles are trained to run after rabbits. A rabbit will circle around and come back to where it started. Our beagles were trained to follow the perfect distance behind them and to always come when they were called.

When I was about eleven we had a beagle named J.D. I helped train him with my dad. We went out one Saturday to hunt by a sandpit outside of town. It was a cold, fall day, but I remember it was such a good time with my dad. He loved to be out in the wilderness.

Then, all of a sudden, our dog took off. We saw the deer he was chasing just before they both disappeared through the trees. You can lose a beagle, even a really good one, if it takes off after a deer. The scent is so strong the dog will lose his sense, so intoxicating he'll keep going and forget all his training. When a deer is spooked, it will keep running for miles.

J.D followed that deer and soon they were out of sight.

"J.D!" I screamed as loud as I could at the dog, hoping he'd hear me, and turn away from the sprinting deer.

My dad and I yelled and screamed his name, but he was gone.

"Please, Dad," I was crying. I started to run after J.D. "Please, please, Dad. We *have* to go get him."

"We can't go after him. There was no way that we could catch up with him. He's gone." My Dad was deflated, but stood firmly where he was until I walked back to him.

I sat there for a minute and cried while Dad was silent. I wanted to be mad at my dad for not running after J.D., but I knew he was right. We'd never have caught up with him.

"Bob," Dad had an idea. "This is what we'll do. I'll put my coat down in the ditch. When J.D. tires out, he'll remember us. He'll come back to this place. He doesn't know how to find his way home from wherever he is, but he'll know how to find his way back here. And if he finds my coat, if he sees it here, then he'll wait here for us."

I frowned through my tears. "Come on, Dad! That's not going to work."

My dad took off his coat on that crisp fall day and wrapped it up in a circle around the rabbit hole we had been watching. It was a brown canvas coat, soft and well worn. It was monumental for him to set down his hunting coat on the ground and drive away from it. When you work for an hourly wage at a warehouse and are supporting five kids, two with special needs, it is not a small gesture to wrap up your favorite coat in a ditch in the hope that your son's dog will see it as a sign that you're coming back for him.

As we drove back the next day, my face was pressed against the cold window, straining to catch a glimpse of my dog. There he was, cuddled up in the middle of the coat. You could see the white and brown ears resting on the elbow patch of the coat sleeve.

I didn't even wait for Dad to park the car. I opened the door and jumped out. "J.D.! Dad, you were right! Dad! He came back! J.D. knew we would come back for him!" J.D.'s entire body shook as he wagged his tail, and I hugged him and cried again in that ditch.

The editor for the Post Crescent heard about it at a card party and interviewed my dad. He did a big write-up about him for the newspaper. That's my dad. He didn't graduate from high school, but he was a very wise man. My dad mentored me through many life experiences like this.

#RichMelheim

In Luke, Jesus tells a story that is often called "The Prodigal Son."

The story involves a son who left home with his inheritance money and squandered it away on reckless living. When he was penniless he decided to return home.

Maybe you've heard someone called a *prodigal* before. When I've heard the word *prodigal* used, it always seems to mean *someone who isn't doing the right thing. Someone who is lost.*

Sometimes Christian parents will refer to a child as a *prodigal*, meaning the child has set out on their own path. They are *wandering* or *lost.*

But that's not what the word means. The word prodigal comes from an old English word that means "lavish." Prodigal means recklessly or with abandon. Jesus didn't call this story "The Prodigal Son." It has earned the name more recently, probably because the younger son spent his money recklessly.

He squandered his wealth in wild living.

He lived lavishly and imprudently, so when a severe drought hit the land, he ended up destitute. He found a job feeding pigs, but he was not even allowed to eat their slop.

One day, this son had a memory of his father's house. He remembered that even the servants in his home lived better than this.

"How many of my father's hired servants
have food to spare, and here I am
starving to death!"

He decided he would go home and ask his father for his forgiveness and for a job in his house. Jesus continues the story this way,

> *"When he was still a long way off, his father saw him and was filled with compassion; he ran to his son, threw his arms around him and kissed him."*

When he was a *long way off*, his father was filled with compassion.

Filled with…

Rage?

Righteous indignation?

No, his father was filled with compassion.

The world is full of droughts and famines, literally and figuratively. Most people come to the end of themselves at some point. As that happens to the next generation, as they find themselves starving for something that really satisfies, where will they turn? If they find themselves surrounded by pigs, what will they remember? What memory will pop up in their heads that will beckon them home?

Many have not grown up in church and do not have a memory of God's House, as it's called. They have no memory of the *Father's House*.

Many who do have childhood memories of church can't recall in those memories the picture of a loving Father. They might think it's not a place worth heading back to.

The memory that urges the son to return home is a recollection of his father's servants.

> *"How many of my father's hired servants have food to spare, and here I am starving to death!"*

What if the way our children remembered our churches had more to do with how well respected the janitor was and less to do with our fancy power point? What if our children grew up with the deep impression that the fast food worker taking our order for a burrito after church is as valuable to God as the pastor we buy lunch for? What if, when our children are knocked to their knees by ill-conceived choices, or unfair markets, or famines, or pig-farmers, they knew there could still be a place for them in the place Jesus promised to prepare? As Jesus described it, "in my Father's House." And once there, they would have food to spare.

If we are looking out at the pig sties and prodigals of the world, wondering why they don't come home, we should consider carefully who is really welcome inside the walls of our churches. And we should also remember that we ourselves are often just as prodigal as the most prodigal, and often just as self-righteous as the older son.

When the prodigal in Jesus' story decided to come home, it wasn't a church he was returning to, it was his actual father's house.

It was the home he grew up in.

How are known sinners treated in your home?

How are your servants treated in your home?

Maybe you don't have any servants, but do you ever hire people to do things for you? Have you ever paid for a meal in a restaurant? Did a server bring you food? Do you pay someone to fix your garage door when it breaks? To install your water heater?

Society doesn't call them "servants" anymore, but I

don't think I need to dig into the Latin root words to explain the connection between the word "servant" and the words "service industry" or "servers". We still pay people to serve us.

In this country, even people *in service industries* pay others for services. Someone takes our order. Someone scans our groceries. Those *someones* are real people who we ought to treat like real people, even when they are working for us. We can look them in the eyes. We can get off our phones. We might not hold the power in our hands to make sure they have food to spare. But at minimum, it's within our power to treat people in the service industry with respect.

If we only focus on loving *our own* kids, and passing on Jesus' love to *our family*, we are not passing on the genuine love of Jesus. Our kids, though they may enjoy being the center of our world now, will eventually see that a self-centered love rings hollow.

God is love, and exists in a perfect, loving relationship. The Creator, the Son and the Spirit existed in this mystical relationship before time. Before space. Before mass. Before energy. God didn't create the world to fulfill an inner loneliness. God created the world because real love doesn't just turn in on itself. Real love creates. Real love multiplies. God has been calling humankind to multiply ever since.

If the prodigal son had remembered a home where his father neglected or abused his children, that would not have been inviting either. As a parent we have a unique relationship with our children that requires a unique love and commitment. Yes, our families need to be healthy. But our families don't need to be healthy *before we do anything else.*

Part of being a healthy family is actively participating in the greater community.

Sometimes we make the mistake of thinking that our physical home, still perhaps decorated with posters of our children's youth, is the place that our dear children must return to, hat in hand, asking for forgiveness.

But what if, like Bob's family beagle, a child can't find their way home?

Bob did everything he could to call him back, but J.D. was gone. Bob couldn't force J.D. to stop chasing the deer.

Bob's dad left a monument in that place. He left his jacket as a sign for the beagle that they'd be coming back for him.

What in our lives left such a scent of home? What if people could know who we are and whose we are and where we belong just by being near us?

What can you do so that when you can't go after your kids, you know they have a place they can come back to? ? What could be the sign of God's loving "scent" and presence for your kids?

What if, when our children were *a long way off*, we *ran to them, threw our arms around them and kissed them* before we even heard what they were coming to say?

What does *a long way off* look like today? One of my friends met a mother who spent her Christmas vacation in Los Angeles, not taking in warm beaches and studio tours, but walking the streets and checking homeless shelters to find her daughter who had run away.

Another friend took a week-long trip just to be near

his son who had recently moved out of state. The son already knew the long list of things his father wished he wasn't doing, the ways he was living recklessly.

The dad didn't come to remind him, but rather, came to *throw his arms around his son*. To treat him to a *fattened calf* (or, *carne asada,* as the locals called it). To spend a week together, meeting his kid's friends. To spend a week playing, talking, giving back rubs, laughing. To bring Easter baskets from Mom. And, yes, to do some crying and praying back at the hotel room.

This dad turned that trip into a well-worn coat with patched-up elbows that smells of a dad who loves you, not because of what you do, but because he's just your dad. A dad who keeps coming back to lay down his coat in a place where you'll be able to find it, if you want to.

We've spent a lot of time in this book talking about how formative the childhood years are, but after <18> is not too late. We don't want you to ever give up on your kids, on your people. God has never given up on us. No matter how old or young our kids are, we can create a home where they are always loved and always welcomed.

Our God is the Prodigal Father in this story we call history, offering *reckless*, *extravagant* love and forgiveness.

Be a prodigal parent. Prodigal isn't a bad word. It's a good word that was used for a bad thing. A lot like us. Let's claim it, rename it, and reframe it.

In a nutshell:

Be a prodigal parent: Love extravagantly. Love lavishly.

EPILOGUE

#RichMelheim

In Deuteronomy, Moses stood at the edge of the Promised Land and spoke his last words to the children of Israel before they went on without him.

Do you know what the religion was in the Promised Land? It was a fertility cult of child sacrifice and temple prostitutes. Do you remember Molek and the child sacrifices? That's the religion in the new neighborhood. *Welcome to your new home in the land of Canaan! Be sure to be a good citizen and sacrifice your children. Then go visit the temple prostitutes every spring to bring on new flocks and herds.* Imagine sending your beloved family into that land. Well, maybe it doesn't take too much imagination.

It used to be that your kids would have to go outside of the house to get in trouble, but today trouble is looking for them on the internet.

We don't have actual child sacrifice, but we are sacrificing our children to many gods. Some of them are good gods, like football, soccer, and hockey. I come from Minneapolis. We have the Mall of America, temple to a lesser god, where there are more cars on a Sunday morning than the ten biggest mega churches put together. We sacrifice our children all the time.

Moses spent his entire life getting the Israelites safely to a land where he would not be able to join them. Think about that. If you had spent your entire ministry trying to get people right to the edge of the Promised Land and you know you aren't allowed to go in.

Think of these words in Deuteronomy 6 as Moses' last words. This is the last shot he gets. This is his legacy. He can't go in with them, but he can send something with them that will give them victory.

If you were on your deathbed, what would you say?

Moses said, "These commandments that I give you today are to be on your hearts. Impress them on your children."

If you look at Jesus' last words before he ascended into heaven, he said, to paraphrase,"Go into all the world and proclaim the Gospel, baptizing them in the name of the Father, Son, and Holy Spirit. *Teaching them to observe all that I have commanded you* and I am with you always." The same words!

Teach them everything God said. Teach your children, and your children's children, Moses says. Teach them in your home town, Jesus says, and in your neighboring towns, and teach them at the ends of the earth.

That's what we want to do.

We might not be on our deathbeds yet, but in our last words in this letter to you, we say: Go. Pass this Good News onto the Next Generation.

Actually, the words in this book came very close to being our last words. When we drove in the car together in Colorado, not long after discussing Moses' last words, we came around a curvy mountain pass at the same moment that a box truck, driving on the opposite side of the road, rounded the turn and slipped just off the edge of the road, tipping onto its two outside wheels for a heart-stopping moment before it steadied and continued safely past us.

We both yelled out as we saw it happen in front of us. If the truck had actually fallen over, it could easily have continued its momentum into our path. We, in that narrow mountain pass, had nowhere to turn. Likely, Bob would not have even had time to react.

A few hours later, we realized that our families might have just been getting notified of the accident. It was sobering.

Bob said, "I really feel like I've put it all on the line, but now, I feel that way even more. Let's just go for it. Let's not leave anything on the table."

If that had been the end, we would have been okay with these being our last words. We're going to just keep talking about this until it is our time to say goodbye anyway. We want you to know the good news.

And if you know it, we want you to help us share it. Share it in Jerusalem, or Lincoln, Nebraska. Share it in your home. Share it with your kids and your friends and your co-workers.

This isn't something hyper-spiritual. It isn't for the paid pastor. It shouldn't be outsourced. It's for every one of us, starting with Mom and Dad, Grandma and Grandpa, and anyone who is putting the babies to bed. That's not just what we want to do. That's who we are. We want you to join us in sharing Christ with everyone, starting with every night in every home.

And if we die tomorrow, we can live with that.

WE WANT YOU TO JOIN US IN SHARING CHRIST WITH EVERYONE, STARTING WITH EVERY NIGHT IN EVERY HOME.

AND IF WE DIE TOMORROW, WE CAN LIVE WITH THAT.

A FREE ONE-YEAR WEEKLY BIBLE SCHEDULE IN SONGS AND GAMES

Faith Inkubators presents a simple and fun way to engage in Scriptures with your family every night. Start by sharing highs and lows, then grab your Bibles to read and highlight the suggested weekly theme verses. Next, hop online to www.faithink.com and enter the suggested FINKlink Code (right columns below). There you'll find Scripture in song, art, games and American Sign Language. Rather than reading a different verse each night during your FAITH5 time, the best brain research would suggest you stick to the same Scripture all week long. By the end of the week, you will know God's Word by heart in both song and sign language. And you'll have it in your mind for the rest of your life!

Check out more on how to implement FAITH5 at www.faith5.org in creative ways and download free samples of the FAITH5 curriculum resources for church and home at www.faithink.com.

For now, enjoy a year's worth of free nightly Scriptures in song, sign language and games using the links on the next 4 pages.

Getting Started: Intro to FAITH5™

Week	Theme	Verse	FINKlink Code
1	Sleep in Peace (Introduction)	Psalm 4:8	SI01
2	Where Can I Go? (Share)	Psalm 139:7	SI15
3	Word in My Heart (Read)	Psalm 119:11,8, 105; 122:1	SI14
4	Keep These Words (Talk)	Deuteronomy 6:4-10	BM15
5	As I Pay My Vows (Pray)	Psalm 61:1-5,8	SI10
6	The Lord Bless You (Bless)	Numbers 6:24-26	BM13

FAITH5 Unit 1: The Books of Moses

Week	Theme	Verse	FINKlink Code
7	Let There Be Light	Genesis 1:1-3	BM01
8	Where Are You?	Genesis 3:8-9	BM03
9	Bow in the Clouds	Genesis 9:13-15,7; 8:22	BM03
10	Look To Heavens	Genesis 15:5	BM04
11	God Will Provide	Genesis 22:1-3a,6-8	BM05
12	Jake's Dream	Genesis 28:11-14	BM06
13	Son of His Old Age	Genesis 37:3-4, 23-24,28,34-35; 50:20a	BM07
14	Burning Bush	Exodus 3:1-2,6-7,11,13	BM08
15	Take a Lamb	Exodus 12:3,5a,6b-7,12-13	BM09

16	Into the Sea	Exodus 15:1-2,9-12	BM10
17	I Am	Exodus 20:2-3	BM11
18	You Shall Be Holy	Leviticus 19:2b; 10:3	BM12
19	Will He Not?	Numbers 23:19	BM14

FAITH5 Unit 2: Into the Promised Land

Week	Theme	Verse	FINKlink Code
20	Be Strong!	Joshua 1:5b,9	PL01
21	As for Me	Joshua 24:15	PL02
22	Hear, O Kings	Judges 5:3	PL03
23	Where You Go	Ruth 1:16	PL04
24	God Looks on the Heart	1 Samuel 16:7	PL05
25	Goliath's Requiem	1 Samuel 17:45-46a,47b	PL06
26	David Danced	2 Samuel 6:14; 22:1-20	PL07
27	Solomon's Prayer	1 Kings 8:27,30	PL08
28	I Know Your Rising	2 Kings 19:27a	PL09
29	Declare His Glory	1 Chronicles 16:24,31-34	PL10
30	If My People	2 Chronicles 7:14	PL11
31	For He Is Good	Ezra 3:10-11b	PL12
32	Strengthen My Hands	Nehemiah 6:9c	PL13
33	The Deep Things	Job 11:7-12	PL15
34	He Has Done It	Psalm 22:27,29-31	SI0
35	O Taste and See	Psalm 34:4-8	SI06
36	A Thousand Years	Psalm 90:4-5,9-10,12	SI11

FAITH5 Unit 3: The Good News

Week	Theme	Verse	FINKlink Code
37	In the Beginning	John 1:1-5,9-12,14	GN01
38	Magnify the Lord	Luke 1:47-49	GN02
39	Emmanuel	Matthew 1:20b-23	GN03
40	Prepare the Way	Matthew 3:1-3	GN04
41	Salt of the Earth	Matthew 5:3-10,13a,14,16	GN05
42	Living Water	John 4:13-15; 7:38b	GN06
43	The Lord's Prayer	Matthew 6:9-13	GN07
44	Love the Lord	Mark 12:28-31a	GN08
45	Are You the One?	Matthew 11:3-5	GN09
46	I Am the Way	John 14:6	GN10
47	Love One Another	John 15:12-13	GN11
48	For God So Loved	John 3:16	GN12
49	Easter Morning	Mark 16:2-7	GN13
50	Stay With Us	Luke 24:29-32	GN14
51	Go Therefore	Matthew 28:19-20	GN15
52	You Will Receive Power	Acts 1:8	GN15

The FAITH5™ (Faith Acts In The Home)

- STEP 1: SHARE your highs and lows every night
- STEP 2: READ a key Bible verse or story every night

- STEP 3: TALK about how your highs and lows relate to that Scripture every night
- STEP 4: PRAY for one another's highs and lows every night
- STEP 5: BLESS one another every night

Does the FAITH5™ work? Go to www.faith5.org and you'll see stories of families who tried it for 6 weeks with amazing results, including:

- A couple with a daughter who couldn't sleep through the night after the murder of her classmate.
- A woman knifed and left for dead by a husband with bipolar disorder as their two little girls slept in the house.
- An autistic boy who needed routine to feel secure.
- A man who gave up on God as a child due to an abusive father, and later came back to God when his own little boy experienced a rare and deadly cancer.
- A single African American army veteran mother with two teens who "adopted" a stray white kid and now Skypes him into her family to share and pray every night.

- A man whose father came back from dementia to bless him right before he died

BIBLIOGRAPHY

1. *Evangelism Is Most Effective Among Kids.* **The Barna Group.** Ventura, CA : The Barna Group, 2004, Research Releases in Family & Kids. *www.barna.com.*

2. **Brown, H. Douglas.** *Principles of Language and Learning and Teaching.* s.l. : Pearson Education, 2000.

3. *Research Shows That The Spiritual Maturity Process Should Start at a Young Age.* **The Barna Group.** 2003, Family & Kids. *www.barna.com.*

4. **The Jason Foundation.** http://jasonfoundation.com/prp/facts/youth-suicide-statistics/. [Online] [Cited: April 6, 2017.]

5. **CDC.** *Suicide Facts at a Glance 2015.*

6. **Chalabi, Mona.** https://fivethirtyeight.com/datalab/how-many-times-the-average-person-moves/. *fivethirtyeight.com.* [Online] January 29, 2015. [Cited: April 10, 2017.]

7. **Long, Heather.** money.cnn.com/2016/04/12/news/economy/millennials-change-jobs-frequently/. *money.cnn.com.* [Online] April 12, 2016. [Cited: April 10, 2017.]

8. **Nouwen, Henri.** Moving from Solitude to Community to Ministry. *Leadership Journal.* Spring, 1995.

9. **Lewis, C. S.** https://www.brainyquote.com/quotes/quotes/c/cslewis105239.html. *BrainyQuote.com.* [Online] Xplore, Inc. [Cited: April 10, 2017.]

10. **Basho, Matsuo.** https://www.brainyquote.com/quotes/quotes/m/matsuobash107176.html. *BrainyQuote.com.* [Online] Xplore, Inc, 2017. [Cited: April 10, 2017.]

ABOUT THE AUTHORS

Bob Lenz

Bob Lenz is an international speaker and author who shares his message with half a million people each year through community outreaches, festivals, school assemblies and conferences. A storyteller at heart, Bob combines personal experience with biblical knowledge to awaken understanding and inspire others to embrace faith in Christ.

Bob is known for his highly sought-after school program called Dignity Revolution. This comprehensive educational series includes school assemblies, teacher in-service training, national pledge, book and a curriculum for grades 6-12. The purpose of the Dignity Revolution is to promote the worth, value, and dignity of every person.

Bob Lenz is founder and president of Life Promotions, a national evangelistic event-based ministry whose mission is to instill hope in youth. Life Promotions is known for Lifest, one of the nation's largest Christian music festivals. The ministry also plans Quake events which are retreats designed to help youth connect with God and one another. To find out more or to support the mission of Life Promotions, visit LifePromotions.com.

Rich Melheim

Dr. Rich Melheim is founder of Faith Inkubators (*www.faithink.com*), the Cross+Generational Ministry Movement (www.crossgenlife.org) and www.richlearning.com. An entrepreneur, author, cartoonist, comedian, publisher, songwriter, family systems guru, business systems consultant, log cabin builder, Rich is also an amateur neurologist and a pretty good dad.

Rich has taught in 1000 cities on five continents, written and produced 7 musical comedy plays including www.lutherthemusical.com, authored 24 books, produced 24 music albums, created an international preschool education experiment, and appeared on 50 network television news shows from WNBC-NY to KTLA to CNN consulting on family issues.

Rich is ordained Lutheran pastor with a BA in Journalism, an MDiv in Theology, and a doctorate the a branch of linguistic philosophy studying meaning (that's "Semiotics").

He has been married to his Bible Camp sweetheart, Arlyce, since 1978, and is the dad of Kathryn and Joseph, two delightful "twenty-somethings" who regularly make him glad to be alive.

Jenica Halula

"Nica" is a writer, film producer, and improv comedian, but she began her career as professional juggler. She began performing at the age of 13 with the Fitz Family, a traveling, real-life family juggling act. She spent the next decade performing improv, writing comedy, and producing short films with HappyFunTime Industries. She now creates story-driven projects for non-profits like Compassion International, award-winning educational videos distributed by Discovery Education, and writing and illustrating stories for adults and kids. Nica lives in Los Angeles with her husband, writer and director, Wes Halula. Occasionally they get to collaborate on projects together, but none yet have turned out as great as their two kids. Jenica is a little bit Millennial, a little bit Gen-X, and totally a parent in the middle of what <18> means: passing on our faith on to the next generation. You can keep up with Nica at TheyGrowOnTrees.com.